A HISTORY OF NAGAS AND NAGALAND

(Dynamics of Oral Tradition in Village Formation)

A HISTORY OF NAGAS AND NAGALAND

(Dynamics of Oral Tradition in Village Formation)

Visier Sanyu

COMMONWEALTH PUBLISHERS
NEW DELHI (INDIA)

A History of Nagas and Nagaland

Edition : 2026

ISBN 81-7169-369-5

Published by **:**
COMMONWEALTH PUBLISHERS (P) LTD.
4831/24, Govind Lane,
Ansari Road, Darya Ganj,
New Delhi - 110002
Ph. : 23272541, 23242541
e-mail : commonwealthpublishers2016@gmail.com

Distributed by :
ARJUN PUBLISHING HOUSE
4831/24, Govind Lane,
Ansari Road, Darya Ganj,
New Delhi - 110002
Ph. : 23272541, 23242541
e-mail : arjunbooks2001@gmail.com

Laser Typesetting by :
Dimple Computers
Delhi

Printed at :
Divine Digital Press
Delhi

Dedicated
to
Indigenous Societies
of the World

Acknowledgement

It Was the trainning in village life which I received during my formative years that sparked my interest and appreciation for things indigenous. I am deeply indebted to my village, Khonoma, where I was born and brought up for imbedding in me the traditional values and fostering insights which sowed seeds for the begining of this work.

Hundreds of Angami villagers and elders spent long hours with me relating ancient tales and traditions which have proved valuable in compiling this book. I owe my thanks to all of them. To my father, THEYIEVIZO, a great story-teller, I am especially indebted. His deep and real knowledge of my people which made him an authority on village traditions has been a real source of inspiration.

The idea of this book emerged out of my doctoral thesis *History of Village formation Among The Angami Nagas : A Case Study of Kohima And Khonoma Villages* For That I thank my supervisor, Prof. J.B. Bhattacharjee. I owe a deep debt of gratitude to my friend and Guru, Dr. R.L. Hangloo of Hyderabad University, for his persistent encouragement, and suggestions to write this book. I also thank Prof *Jan Van Sina* of *Wisconson University* for his valuable suggestions.

Finally I owe very special debt to my wife, PARI, because without her constant support and many suggestions for improvement, this book would have not been possible.

Kohima 1995
Nagaland

VISIER SANYU

Contents

1

INTRODUCTION

It is now widely established that there is a missing chapter in world history—the history of the indigenous people. History has been the study of the growth of nation states, of imperialism, colonialism, 'civilization', Marxism, and ideologies of all shades and colours. For the last two decades, however, the indigenous peoples all over the world are asserting their right of place in the world community and are becoming equal partners in shaping the future course of history. It is significant that the United Nations declared 1993 as the International Year of the Indigenous People, and further declared 1994-2004 as the International Decade of Indigenous People. This Decade could be an important landmark in the history of mankind.

But the study of indigenous history has not so far received the adequate attention of scholars, and this serious neglect cannot be attributed to them alone. One has to appreciate the equally serious lack of knowledge in handling the subject because of an unfamiliarity with the dynamics of a methodology geared to probe and understand this aspect.

Reconstructing the history of societies dispossessed of any written records is an extremely difficult task requiring unique and unconventional methodology geared to meet this particular problem. In spite of all the difficulties however, methodologies such as that developed by Jan Vansina have proved useful in understanding such societies. To quote Vansina,

> "Whether memory changes or not, culture is reproduced by remembrance put into words and deeds. The mind through memory carries culture from generation to generation. How it is possible for a mind to remember and out of nothing to spin complex ideas messages and instructions for living which manifest continuity over time is one of the greatest wonders one can study, comparable only to human intelligence and thought itself. Oral tradition should be central to students of ideology, of society, of psychology, of art, and finally, of history."[1]

Jan Vansina has brilliantly demonstrated the pertinence of the oral approach to areas where very little exists in terms of written source materials. His efforts in reconstructing the history of the kingdoms of Savanna depended primarily on hearsay, visions, dreams, hallucinations verbal art, personal traditions, traditions of origin and genesis, epics tales, proverbs, sayings, memorized speeches and so on.[2] He believes that "traditions are perfectly congruent with the society. Any alteration in social organization or practice is immediately accompanied by a corresponding alteration in tradition."[3]

There are various theoretical attempts to characterize the Nagas, but the generally accepted view is that they are a powerful indigenous nation consisting of about 40 tribes or

---

1. Jan Vansina, *Oral Tradition as History*, Wisconsin, 1985, p. xi.
2. Jan Vansina, *Kingdoms of the Savanna*, Wisconsin, 1975.
3. Jan Vansina, *op.cit.*, p. 120.

sub-nations that have for centuries inhabited the Naga Hills at the tri-junction of China, India and Myanmar. Their home is the meeting place of the so-called brown and yellow races of Asia. Their intruiging history and culture has always baffled western scholars. According to Julian Jacobs, "Here was a culture which might provide clues to the great movements in human history".[4]

The Angami, a prominent tribe of the Nagas, occupy the heart of Naga ancestral domain. Although the Angami were one of the earliest settlers here, there is an extreme paucity of written records on them. The only authoritative work exclusively focussing on them has been left by J.H. Hutton, who served as an administrator in Naga Hills from 1917 - 1935.[5] Hutton tried his best to include all aspects of Angami work in his account, but when the question of singling out the essential features of their life arises, his account reveals certain inadequacies which probably can be attributed to his colonial culture and his ties with the government he came to represent. However, his account continues to retain its significance particularly for those who are still unfamiliar with the Angami Naga.

The application of oral tradition varies from place to place. While pursuing this study, detailed work and interviews of the older generation and traditional story tellers was conducted. This stock of folk tales, poems, legends, sayings, prayers and proverbs has not only enriched our understanding of this phenomenon but has also urged us as to which question to pursue. The various festive occasions and traditional performances were also carefully observed to yield the analysis. At the same time, it

4. Julian Jacobs, in *Nagaland : A Contemporary Ethnography,* Editor: Subhadra Channa, Delhi, 1992, p. 297.

5. J.H. Hutton, *The Angami Nagas,* London, 1921.

has not been possible to go into analysis in detail and some aspects will remain unsettled at this stage. Since this work has been a micro-level enquiry and only two villages have been chosen for study, discussion with regard to politico-judicial, ideological and superstructural aspects remains limited particularly during the pre-colonial times.

It needs to be further specified that attempts have been made to avoid reduction of analysis of the proposed aspects solely to the definitions of the mode of production which would possibly have led to widen the basic dialectical unity but dismiss the importance of the socio-economic formation as a coherent of social organism. Generally, the process of the origin of the Angami Nagas has been examined with a view that all cultures have taken elements from other cultures. Various changes were effected through borrowing concepts and practices and migration of families from village to village.

The objectives of the British in subduing the Angami and the process involved in their subjugation has been illustrated with different variables, that is, force, persuasion, role of missionary activity and the nature of the self determination of the Nagas. An estimate of the representatives of colonialism *vis-a-vis* the Angami Nagas is also accounted with the idea of observing transition and transformation which has been further taken up while viewing the nature and process of modernization.

All these concepts have been based on the empirical studies of two villages of KOHIMA and KHONOMA—two prominent Angami seats. The understanding that these two Angami villages show—a considerable degree of peculiarity in their varied phases of transition and transformation forms—the basic discussion in this book.

2

MIGRATION AND SETTLEMENT

The migration of peoples and tribes has been an important aspect in history since the very inception of human society. There has been migration from one country to another and from one continent to another. This movement has always shaped and reshaped human history. In the European continent, the Germanic and Celtic tribes crossed over to Rome and laid the foundation of early medieval society in Europe.[1] A classical example of the history of migration was that of the *Maori* people who migrated from *Havaiki* in the Eastern Pacific to *Aotearao*—"Land of the Long White Clouds"—which later became New Zealand when the Europeans migrated to the islands and defeated the Maoris.[2] India also has its long has history of migrations.

---

1. Perry Anderson, *Passages form Antiquity to Feudalism*, E.A. Thompson, *The Barbarian Kingdom in Gaul and Spain*, Medieval Studies, Vol. viii, Nottingham, 1963, p. ii.
2. Robert Paul Jordan, "New Zealand: The Last Utopia?" in *National Geographic*, Vol. 171, No. 5, May, 1987. The history of the *Maori* people was also told to the author by *Te Rangi Huata*, a *Maori* from New Zealand. *Havaiki* was a legendary island which no longer exists, but the famous voyage of the *Maoris* by canoes formed an interesting part of the *Maori* history of New Zealand.

Aryans crossed over from Central Asia and settled in India.[3]

The non-Aryans came both before and after the Aryans to the Indian sub-continent. The non-Aryans who were in mainland India before the advent of the Aryans are generally described as aborigines, but their ancestors too must have migrated to India in different phases. The social categories described as tribal had also migrated in various streams. There are varied definitions of 'tribe', but the generally accepted version is that it is a small group of people who can trace their origins to a common ancestry, possessing a communal social organization peculiar to their custom and tradition, and remaining integrated because of their singular ethnicity. These days they are also described as indigenous. There is evidence to show that some of the tribes of non-Aryans origin migrated to India much before the arrival of the Aryans. In the Indian context, the North Westen and North Eastern frontiers have been the main entry points from very early times.

On the North Eastern Frontier, we find that the *Boros* were one of the first major groups who migrated to the plains of Assam. Their language was fundamentally Tribeto-Burman. The other early groups which, perhaps, preceded them were speakers of the Austric group of languages. They may have been akin to the present *Khasis*.[4]

---

3. J.W. McCrindle, *Ancient India as Described by Megasthenes*, edited by R.C. Jain, Delhi, 1972, pp. XIII-XLVI.
   See also his appendix 4, pp. 235-236.
   R.C. Majumdar, *Ancient India*, Delhi, 1971 (6th revised edition), pp. 29-32.
4. Rashid Yusuf Ali, administrator and scholar, who has studied the migration of indigenous to the North Eastern region, was kind enough to provide materials and information on the subject. See also W.W. Hunter, *A Statistical Account of Assam*, in two Vols., Delhi, 1975 (reprint).

Those tribes who came after these early groups and settled in this region were the various tribes of *Koch, Hajong, Dalu, Garo, Mikir, Dimasa, Arleng, Chutiya, Moram, Lalung, Rabha, Mech, Adi, Apatani, Mishing, Nishi, Ahom, Singpho, Khamti, Kuki, Mizo, Naga, Meitei* and so on.[5]

The Nagas who settled in the Naga Hills have various theories of their migration, often recorded by foreign writers. However, the earliest specific reference to the Nagas was made by Claudius Ptolemy in 150 A.D. in his Geographia where he referred to the Naga country as "The Realm of the Naked".[6]

On the basis of language, their origin is assigned by Sir G.A. Grierson to that of the Tibeto-Burmans, who came with the second wave of migration from North Western China between the upper waters of the Yangtse-Kiang and Hoang-Ho rivers. According to Grierson, the Angami Naga language is of the Tibeto-Chinese family.[7]

Huang Tsang, the Chinese pilgrim who visited Assam during Bhaskarvarman's rule in 645 A.D. said,

> "the east of this country is bounded by a line of hills, so that there is no great city to the kingdom. The frontiers are contiguous to the barbarians of south-west China. These tribes are in fact akin to those of the Man people in their customs."[8]

Ahom Buranjees also recorded that by the time the Ahoms came to Assam in the thirteenth century, Nagas were already settled in Naga Hills. They wrote of Naga resistance

5. Asoso Yonuo, *The Rising Nagas*, Delhi, 1974, pp. IX-X.
6. Claudius Ptolemy, *Geographia VII*, ii, p. 18
   The orginal text is in Greek:.
7. G.A. Grierson, *Linguistic Survey of India*, Vol. III, Part II, Varanasi, 1903, p. 11.
8. Thomas Watters, *On Yuan Chwang's Travels in India*, (A.D. 629-645), London, 1904, Delhi, 1973 (reprint) p. 186.

to Sukapha, the founder of Ahom Kingdom.[9] Of course, the exact date of the arrival of the Nagas into the Naga Hills cannot be established with precision, but at the same time their entrance before the Christian Era cannot be ruled out.

While discussing the history of Naga migration there emerge some important questions:

(*a*) What was the original home of the Nagas before migrating to the Naga Hills?

(*b*) What are those circumstances that forced them to migrate from their original homeland?

(*c*) What was the nature and route of migration?

The sources do not provide the exact answers to all these questions at present but some of the legends, folktales and mythology examined with the help of the oral approach, do help to a great degree in solving these problems. Due to the lack of written or recorded sources it makes it exceedingly difficult to analyse the history of the Nagas particularly for the pre-British period. However, the indigenous societies had their own ways of recording events from generation to generation through professional storytellers. It is the information extracted from them which lends credence to our analysis.

Basically, for much of its history, South East Asia has been oriented towards the two great world cultures—China on one hand, India on the other. In South East Asia, the earliest settlers were Paleolithic or pre-Paleolithic food-gatherers, hunters, fishers and folk who had not made the transition to a stone-using culture.[10] The units of this social organization seem to have been small. Often the hunting group or the clan, though in its infancy, were nomadic in

---

9. E.A. Gait, *A History of Assam*, Calcutta, 1967 (reprint), pp. 78-79. P. Gogoi, *The Tai and the Tai Kingdom*, Gauhati, 1968, pp. 256-258.
10. Williams Watson, *China Before The Han Dynasty*, London, 1961, pp. 22-54.

habit and generally moved in a defined hunting territory. A traditional division of labour existed between the sexes. The men concentrated on hunting while the women and children collected insects and vegetables for food. By and large, the people could be labelled as primitive.[11] Yet in some of their practices one can glimpse the beginnings of agriculture. For example, the Semang of Malaya devised a rudimentary form of tree cultivation and put back into the ground the tips of wild yams in order that a fresh crop might grow.[12] Some of the groups did not use hoe or plough but remained satisfied with digging sticks while other groups practised sedentary agriculture with the hoe as the basic implement. In fact, there were racial contacts between these groups in spite of the technological contrasts. Those who practised the more primitive type of agriculture belonged to some of the earlier stock like Negrito and Nesiot, who originally occupied much of the region but who were increasingly displaced by later groups.[13]

In course of time some of the tribes in upland areas inserted themselves into the existing ecological equilibrium

---

11. S.D. Marshall has clearly maintained a distinction between the peasant and primitive. He mentions that "in primitive economies most production is geared to use of producers or to discharge of kinship obligations rather than to exchange and gain. A corollary is that de facto control of means of production is decentralized, local, and familial in primitive society..."
S.D. Marshall, "Political Power and the Economy in Primitive Society" in *Essays in Science of Culture in Honour of Leslie A White*, edited by G.E. Dole and R.L. Carniero, New York, 1960, p. 408.
12. John K. Fairbank, Edwin O. Resichauer, and Albert M. Craig, *East Asia Tradition and Transformation*, London, 1973, p. 18 "Rice, which is the chief cereal of Asia today, is a plant of Southeast Asian origin, and its cultivation was already well established in the Yangtse Valley in pre-historic times".
13. C.P. Fitz Gerald, *A Concise History of East Asia*, London, 1966, pp. 218-236.

and created for themselves a living space with minimum disruption of that equilibrium incapable of mastering nature. There was a passive adjustment to the environment. In generalized terms these groups would not reach the age of stable agricultural systems based on furrowing. The shifting cultivation was more a shifting of fields rather than a shifting of crops. The amount of land for shifting cultivation was not enough to correspond to the growing population. The ratio of agricultural land must have also been maintained at a low rate due to the nature of technology. Keping in view the claims of the clan, the kinship obligations, particularly at a time when everything was to be made from the produce of the land and in view of the primitive agrarian technology and the means of irrigation, there clearly was a low land to man ratio. The growing population pressure necessitated an increasing area of land which caused some of these groups who could not cope with the environment to migrate to other parts in search of more favourable conditions. As this stage the migrants were directed by the intervening barriers of mountains and jungles southwards along the seaways of the Malayan world.[14] The other factor which added to this migration within Asia was the expansion of the Chinese Han people pushing southwards as population grew in the cradle area in the valley of the Yellow River. [15] They filled up sub-tropical and tropical China and the pressure of population triggered the momentum which set off great ripples of migration which affected the whole of Asia.[16] As Buchanan remarks :

---

14. C.P. Fitz Gerald, *The Southern Expansion of the Chinese People*, London, 1972.
15. *Ibid.*
16. D.R. Sardesai, *South East Asia—Past and Present*, Delhi, 1981, pp. 7-10.

> "over hundreds of years the pre-Chinese peoples of Central Asia were displaced into the upland areas of Indo-Chinese lands far to the South and their pressure in turn triggered tribal movements which affected the whole of mainland South East Asia and the adjoining island worlds."[17]

These immigrant tribes took different routes. Some took the Himalayan section which extends down through the Patkai, Arakan Yoma, and Banda Arch towards Sumatra and Java, and some took the Pacific section which extends from Formosa through the Phillipines, Borneo and on to Japan.[18]

From the above description it can be argued that perhaps the Nagas were among those tribes who migrated from China through the Patkai section and settled on the way in the Naga Hills. There are living examples to illustrate how during migration some of the tribes broke away and settled down enroute. In Borneo and Formosa, there are some indigenous groups who still have the same traditions, culture, socio-religious organizations as the Nagas in the Naga Hills.[19] Some of the mountain tribes of Vietnam also have much in common with some Naga tribes, particularly in manner of dress and food habits.[20]

---

17. Keith Buchanan, *The South East Asian World,* London, 1967, p. 26.
18. W.C. Smith, *The Ao Naga Tribe of Assam,* London, 1925, pp. 153-160. See also, D.E.G. Hall, *A History of South East Asia,* London, 1958.
19. Keviselie Hans Mathisen, a Sami from Norway has conducted a comparative study of the Nagas and the indigenous of Formosa and found many similarities in cultural and social organizations. He visited both the places in 1977. But unfortunately his travel accounts have not been published. The author of this book met him personally in Norway in 1984 to get this information.
20. The scholar visited South Vietnam in 1974 and met members of the mountain people, and noted certain striking similarities between the two tribes, particularly, some weaving patterns were identical.

The Naga scholar, Horam, has his own views about the original home of his people. He writes:

> "There can be little doubt that at one time the Nagas must have wandered about before they found their permanent abode; from their myths and legends one gathers that there is a dim relationship with the natives of Borneo in that the two have a common traditional way of headhunting; with the Phillipines and Formosa through the common system of terrace cultivation; and with the Indonesians, as both use the loin loom for weaving cloth. The embroidery on the Naga cloths resemble the kind done on Indonesian cloths".[21]

According to the Burma Census Report, successive invasion of Tibeto-Burman peoples came from the region of Western China, between the sources of the Yangtse-Kiang and Hoang-Ho rivers.[22] Marshall writes:

> "the early home of the people of Eastern Asia was in the upper reaches of Hoang-Ho or the Yellow River of China and that from this centre the Tibetans moved westwards; the early tribes of Indo-China southwards; and the Chinese south-eastwards. According to this view the proginators of the Karen probably formed a part of their southward migration".[23]

Another Naga Scholar Alemchiba, says:

> "We can conclude that, the original stock starting from the centre of dispersion in Sikiang Province first moved westernly and upon reaching the headwaters of Irrawady and Chindwin rivers, bifurcated into several directions, ultimately leading to Tibet, to Assam, to the hill ranges between Assam and Burma. That branch which came to

---

21. H. Horam, *Naga Policy*, Delhi, 1975, p. 28.
22. *Burma Census Report of 1911*, p. 252.
23. *Ibid.*, p. 6. The Karens of Burma are closely related to the Nagas.

> the hill range moved further west and entered Naga Hills. Another wave from South East Islands taking a north-westerly direction and entered Naga Hills using Burma as a corridor".[24]

Another scholar whom we have referred to earlier is Hutton. He worte:

> "The history of how the Naga tribes came precisely to occupy their present position has, of course, passed into the dim obscurity of vague traditions. But enough of them remain to give some indication of the course which the migration took. The legends of the Aos and of the Semas give those tribes a more or less autochthonous origin, though these legends are probably the old legends of the race which have been given a local value. The Angamis, too, spring from ancestors who emerged from the bowels of the earth, but that not in Angami country, but in some land to the south. And all the weight of tradition points to migration from the south, except in the case of Kacha Naga".[25]

All these observations suggest very important solutions to two aspects: (*a*) the origin of the Nagas, and (*b*) the route of migration. It becomes amply clear that the Nagas came from the Mongolian stock who migrated from China before the Christian Era. This also suggests that the migration of these Nagas did not take place in one wave. It must have continued for some centuries in various groups because the oral sources, folklore and other legendary sources do support us in suggesting that all the Naga tribes did not split up into different tribes only from Naga Hills itself. There are some tribes like *Angami, Sema, Lotha, Rengma,* and *Chakhesang* who

---

24. M. Alemchiba Ao, *A Brief Historical Account of Nagaland*, Kohima, 1970, p. 19.
25. J.H. Hutton, *op.cit.*, p. 6.

have branched out from Khezhakenoma.[26] But there are other tribes too who branched out either enroute to Naga Hills or in their early homeland. The former tradition seems to be more probable, so far as the question of the racial symptoms of the Nagas are concerned, there is no doubt that they are a Mongolian race and a distinct unit in themselves, but the centuries of migration on their route must have certainly brought them into contact not only with some other races but must have also been influenced by their technology and varied social, political, and religio-cultural traditions. To accept Horam's view that they are of a mixed blood and that "no Naga tribe is of pure blood"[27] is historically intelligible. It is difficult to believe that the art of terrace cultivation practised by the Angamis and the *Igorot* of Phillipines is the same and that they could be one as has been put forward by W.C. Smith.[28] The way the art of cultivation is carried out does not always depend on the way man wants to carry it out, but often depends on definite environmental and ecological conditions. Eric Wolf has profoundly established how such environmental factors play a role in evolving a diverse society.

> "Civilization has a long and involed history; the archaeological record indicates a great diversity in the processes which allowed men in different parts of the world to make the transition from primitives to peasants.... From these or similar original centres, cultivation spread out with variable speed in different directions, being adapted to demands of new climates and new social exigencies".[29]

---

26. *Khezhakenoma* is the original home of many Naga tribes. It is named after *Koza* the founder of the village. *Khezhakenoma* villagers still call their villages *Kozami*, which means 'man of Koza'.
Source: from Khezhakenoma villagers tales.
27. H. Horam, *op.cit.*, p. 28.
28. W.C. Smith, *op.cit.*, pp. 153-160.
29. Eric Wolf, *Peasants*, London, 1966, p. 4.

However, the influences of the races they came into contact with cannot be completely ignored.

A thorough examination of sources leads one to believe that the Nagas took the route of the Patkai Himalayan section and it could be possible that some branch of the tribe did not settle in Naga Hills but continued their march to Borneo, Java, Sumatra and the Phillipines. The view that they took the Pacific section and then reached the Naga Hills is not historically convincing and in appropriate.[30] Although the possibility of some branch having taken a different direction through the Pacific cannot be ruled out, yet Alemchiba on the basis of Marshall's view and the Burma Census Report, derives the conclusion which is not far from our view so far as the as the origin of the Naga is concerned.[31]

Apart from this written record as a source material, we have some oral source—folklore, legends and traditions which throw light on the subject of migration. Today, almost all the Naga tribes, trace their origin back to the village of *Khezhakenoma* in Nagaland.[32] *Khezhakenoma* is a village in *Chakhesang* area near the present Manipur border.

---

30. W.C. Smith, *op.cit.*
31. Alemchiba Ao, *op.cit.*, pp. 18-19.
32. The legends of *Khezhakenoma* are very popular in Nagaland. The author met many elders from various villages to get this information during field workd in 1987. It is impossible to mention them all by name but the main informants are the following from *Khezhakenoma*:
From Chisomi clan:
Mr. Vivotso (63), Area Council Member
Mr. Lhouchinyi (61)
Mr. D.K. Ngone (53), Ex-Village Chairman
Mr. Selu (52) Gaon Bura
Mr. Mebemvu (90), the eldest man in the village
From Zeipfemi clan:

(Contd. on next page)

The legend recounts that a person named *Koza* came from the East and after reaching Mekroma (Maikhel) in Manipur he rested for some time and pondered on which way his steps should lead him next. Ultimately, he prayed to his God for guidance. Suddenly a bird flew by and alighted on the horn of his mithun[33] and then flew off again in the direction of *Khezhakenoma*. In order to doubly check this guidance from above, he placed his walking stick on the ground and the stick fell down, pointing in the same direction towards which the bird had flown. *Koza* took this to be direct guidance from the Spirits to continue his journey in that specific direction. He set off for *Khezhakenoma* and upon reaching his destination, legend has it that he saw the very same bird that had appeared to him earlier resting there upon a stone.[34] Later on, *Koza* found that a frog had brought a grain of rice and left it on the Stone where it multiplied into two. *Koza* also brought a basket of rice which doubled when place on the Stone. He

---

(Contd. from previous page)

Mr. Khalo Ladu (58), Area Council member
Mr. C. Kedonyi (52), School Teacher
Mr. Kepfelhou, Gaon Bura
From Komino clan:
Mr. Chelo (64)
Mr. Ngode (75), Ex-Gaon Bura
Mr. Kodova (50), Gaon Bura
Mr. Kevekha Zehol, research scholar NEHU, who also acted as interpreter for the author.

33. *Mithun* is the most valued and prestigious animal among all the Naga tribes. It is the status symbol demonstrating wealth and power. The original word for *mithun* is not known but perhaps originates from the Angami word *mithu* meaning cow. *Bos Frontalis* is its Latin name.
34. According to legend, *Koza* stuck his rod into the ground where it took root and grew into a tree. There is still a tree in *Maikhel* village which is supposed to be an off-shoot of the original tree. This tree is much revered by the people of *Mikhel* because of its connection with *Koza*.

then decided to settle down in *Khezhakenoma* along with his cattle wealth. *Koza* was blessed with sons in course of time. The sons continued the practice of spreading rice on the Sacred Stone. However, one day they began to fight over whose turn it was to spread the rice on the Stone. *Koza's* wife realized then that the Stone would prove to be a bone of contention between her sons. So she lit a great fire under it. The Stone exploded with a mighty sound like thunder, and the Power of the Stone left it and went to Heaven.

Legend traces the growth of *Koza's* people in this land as they prospered and multiplied. It is said that their numbers swelled to seven thousand and resulted in the formation of the seven villages of (1) *Khezhakenoma*, (2) *Tipfolomi*, (3) *Mobvolomi*, (4) *Laculomi*, (5) *Chilhuomi*, (6) *Pfulomi*, and (7) *Chichulomi*. As they increased in number, the land grew too small for them. Thus the people migrated in search of land and food. The people spread out in different directions and formed the different Naga tribes.[35]

Although the legend of *Khezhakenoma* is generally accepted by most of the Naga tribes, *viz., Angami, Chakhesang, Rengma, Sema, Zeliang, Lotha*, etc., some of the other tribes have their own versions and legends. For instance, the *Aos* have a legend that they originated from six stones which were shaped in the form of the male and female human reproductive organs. These stones were from *Chongliyimti*, a village in the *Sangtam* area, where to this day they are located.[36]

A careful examination of these legends and folklore reveals that when the first wave of migration took place, a branch of this Mongoloid race, after taking the Patkain sec-

---

35. This is the original content of the legend as told by the people of *Khezhakenoma*.
36. J.P. Mills, *The Ao Nagas*, London, 1973 (reprint), pp. 1-2.

tion, must have reached Manipur area first after crossing Burma. This assumption can be made in the light of the legends of many Naga tribes in Manipur which refer to *Maikhel* as their original homeland.[37] Although Nagaland does have a direct border with Burma, migration seems to have taken place from the south in Manipur. A possible reason for this could be the course of the Chindwin river which flows southwards towards Manipur where it meets a tributary flowing down from Manipur near *Tammu*, a village in the present Manipur-Burma border. It is most probable that these early groups of migrants used the Chindwin river as their guide since it is the largest river in the region. It therefore is quite probable that while some may have continued southward, others could have settled near the confluence and even followed the tributary northwards through Manipur towards Nagaland. The theory that they followed the course of the Chindwin river is supported by an Angami legend which says that they travelled across "big waters" before they arrived at their present homeland.[38] If this is the migratory route they followed, it would substantiate the theory that the tribes entered Nagaland from the south and not via its northern border.

After entering Manipur, they might have settled in and around *Maikhel*. Since the early tribal community before settling in Naga Hills was pastoral in nature, the settlers would look for land that was conducive to agriculture as well as good for pasture. It is perhaps as a result of this that some branch of the same tribe followed their chief, *Koza*, and left for *Khezhakenoma*. This land must have had considerable attraction for them as it was virgin land before *Koza* arrived.

The legend of the Bird and the Walking Stick could be

---

37. T.C. Hodson, *The Naga Tribes of Manipur*, London, 1911.
38. This legend was told in 1987 by Peselie, an old man of 85 years from Kohima village.

an exaggeration, but it was also a part of the early tradition where everything good or bad was attributed to nature and man was not in a position to be the author of his own actions. As is usual, myths and legends have a tendency to be exaggerated, and here it is interesting to note the mention of *Koza's mithun*. The *mithun* (Bos Frontalis) is a wild bison. The domestication of this wild animal prior to the arrival of *Koza* is most unlikely.

The legend which refers to the Frog, the Sacred Stone, and the Single Grain of Rice which multiplied provides some important clues. That *Koza* and his followers had rice with them could point to a knowledge, on their part, of the art of agriculture. The mention of the frog provides a clue to the nature of the local fauna which in turn would indicate that the land was suitable for their purposes as frogs are generally found in areas which have a good water supply throughout the year. The story of rice multiplying on the Sacred Stone could reflect the fertility of the land they had come to. When *Koza's* group arrived, the general condition of the land—its fertility as well as the pasture land must have induced them to settle there for a while. A careful examination of this site makes it amply clear that what has been referred to as the Sacred Stone is actually a raised platform of stones on which a dolmen was found which is now cracked in several parts.[39] The other probable thesis which can explain the existence of this stone is that since the people of *Koza's* group were not well aware of the ecological and environmental conditions of *Khezhakenoma*, and finding by chance some grains of rice on the rock, they must have deduced that the land was suitable for the cultivation of this crop. The stone may have been used for threshing

39. The exhaustive field work of the author includes his visit of the Sacred Stone of *Koza* in *Khezhakenoma* village.

paddy and that was how some rice was left on it, which would give them this clue. Whatever the possible conjectures, it is as a result of this that the stone is held most sacred. In early times, when society was not yet developed to combat the natural forces with scientific tools and mind because of a lack of knowledge, various spirits and powers were attributed to all the natural forces involved in any economic activity concerning human life.

However, after settling down in *Khezhakenoma*, *Koza's* clan seems to have been placed in a more advantageous position than they were in their previous settlements. On the one hand, they were now possessed with fertile land for settled wet agriculture. On the other hand, the forest areas not only provided wood and cane for their domestic needs but also some land for dry agriculture which could be devoted to cereals, pulses, maize, etc., and the grazing lands to support their cattle. Apart from this the new fauna and flora gava them an added advantage. Birds and animals multiplied in new varieties by cross-breeding and domestication. A living example of this is the *mithun*. This rare animal which is found only in the North Eastern region is the result of domestication of the wild *Bos Frontalis*.

However, gradually, as population went on increasing, *Koza's* generation brought more land under terrace cultivation and supplemented their living by hunting and craft-making. This was the natural and historically inevitable course to follow. What was the nature of this development in settlement and what were the main hindrances will form part of our discussion from here onwards.

Generally, the setting up of human society does not alone depend on the amount of human labour power that will be utilized for various production techniques, but depends much on the ecology, environment and demography of the area they were settling in. It generally depends on the nature of the soil, the capacity of arable land, the availability of forest land, pasture, and other resources of the area. It also has a close relationship with nature and technology.[40]

The examination of the landscape and the ecology of the area clearly reveals that these Naga Hills were rich in forests, pasture and fruits. Besides, there were varieties of wild animals in these thickly wooded forests to support human habitation. Tradition reveals that hunting played an important part in this society. Ritually, hunting and war were closely related. In the Angami language, the two words are synonymous—"*chu-terhu*" literally meaning "hunting-war". But here emerges an important question if this was the case, then why did the transition not take place to another mode of production? Or, why did society continue to remain unchanged in tribal formation?

Our assumption, which is based only on oral information of legends and traditions, is that when some groups first came and settled in *Khezhakenoma* area they started terrace cultivation. But the natural disruption, the backward and primitive technology did not permit them to develop their material resources. Though these tribes were agriculturists and also reared animals, it should be noted that they never utilized their cattle for labour power in agriculture or for transportation. Even when they found some portions of land were favourable to settled agriculture, they still continued to depend on human labour power only. Here, it clearly indicates that this was an important factor which strengthened the tribal social organization based on the communal mode because of the absence of technology and any labour other than their own. As these men were forced to depend on the members of their community, obviously, the division of labour could not grow that fast. The other reason that was responsible for

40. J.D. Bernal, *Science in History*, 4 Vols., London, Vol. 3, pp. 65-81.

such slow growth was that in those early days, their strength and schedule was largely determined by nature.[41]

The lack of labour force did not help them in cultivating their land appropriately and when they were not certain of their one crop economy, they continued to subsist on hunting and food gathering. The other factor was that the area remained completely cut off from the growing influence of the world. The people maintained isolation because the coming of more people would have affected their ethnicity though it would also present its own contribution in various ways. Due to these factors, their material life did not improve much. It also appears that only when the supply of their hunting was almost exhausted, would they start looking for alternate sources of sustenance.

It was this slow pace of development which prolonged the transition from tribal conditions to non-tribal and served to keep tribal ties very strong. When these tribes started looking for alternate avenues of sustenance, they were forced to settle in various sparsely populated settlements within the Naga Hills. It was due to this reason that some went from *Khezhakenoma* to the southern Angami area. This southern Angami group was also known as Zonuo-Keyhonuo.

---

41. Charles Montesquieu rightly believes in the influence of soil and climate on the history of nations. He believes that geographical environment determines men's needs and that these needs in turn determine the laws and usages evolved in one social milieu or another. Montesquieu is right in asserting that the geographical conditions of an area determine the social conditions. But what is wrong with his thesis is that geography alone is insufficient to explain the history of nations, and that the additional objective historical reasons have also their own role to play.
Kh. Monjan, *Landmarks in History*, Moscow, 1979, p. 89.

From the demography of Naga settlement, it seems that a group of people from within the tribe came into conflict with *Koza's* authority in *Khezhakenoma* and that the group went back to Manipur. The migration from *Khezhakenoma* took a serious turn because now we see that generally all who came out from *Koza's* group proceeded in a westerly direction and some towards the north-west of the Naga Hills. One really faces a problem while looking for an answer to the question of why this migration proceeded in two directions only and not to other areas which were supposed to have been equally virgin at the time. Probably one can believe that by the time migration from *Khezhakenoma* took place the Manipuris were already settled in their present homeland. The other reason could be that the northern Naga tribes had also entered into Naga Hills and started spreading in westerly and southwestern directions. Possibly because of this group known as Tenyimia the northern tirbes did not proceed towards the south Naga Hills and in the south-west direction.

It seems that during *Koza's* time clanship or chiefship among the Nagas was deeply rooted and *Koza* appears to have divided areas under his various clanships, like one group which went to Manipur and became *Tangkhuls.*[42] The other tribes which emerged were *Sema,*[43] *Rengma,*[44] *Lotha,*[45] *Zeliang,*[46] *Mao,*[47] *Maram,*[48] and *Angami.*[49] Except for the

42. T.C. Hodson, *op.cit.*
43. J.H. Hutton, *The Sema Nagas*, London, 1921.
44. J.P. Mills, *The Rengma Nagas*, London, 1937.
45. J.P. Mills, *The Lhota Nagas*, London, 1922.
46. Ursula Graham Bowers, *Naga Path*, London, 1950.
47. T.C. Hodson, *op.cit.*
48. *Ibid.*
49. J.H. Hutton, *The Angami Nagas*, *op.cit.*

Tangkhuls, all the others who branched out from *Khezhakenoma* had relationships with Angami which makes it clear that the Tangkhuls who left for Manipur either lost contact with the Angamis or came under the influence of the Meiteis.[50] It could also be possible that during *Koza's* lifetime some sub-clans emerged to control larger areas and after his death they spilt into independent units of full-fledged clans or tribes. Here it should be noted that the formation of these tribes took place much later though the process of migration had set in.[51]

Among these, one group which occupied a village known as *Sumi* became the Sema tribe. Hutton wrote,

> "the Semas point to the south direction from which they came. They relate the story of the *Khezhakenoma* Stone as well as many other folktales common to the Angamis and Lothas, particularly the later. They do not, however, trace their origin south of Mao, but point to Tuhaju (Japvo) as the place from which they sprang. The ancestors of the Sema came from that mountain and the Sema villages spread, according to one account, from Sumi or Somi, a village near Kezabama."[52]

But according to the *Khezhakenoma* version the ancestor of the *Semas* who left *Khezhakenoma* was a man called *Chilo* and his descendants came to be known as *Chimi* from his name and hence the name *Sema*.[53]

As mentioned earlier, one of the groups left *Khezhakenoma* and went to Manipur and settled in a place which has been called *Kozaba* which means 'Koza's place'

50. T.C. Hodson, *The Meitheis*, London, 1908.
51. J.H. Hutton, *The Angami Nagas, op.cit.*, pp. 351-387.
52. J.H. Hutton, *The Sema Nagas, op.cit.*, p. 5.
53. This information was obtained from Khezhakenoma village elders as already referred.

the name of the place which still remains to this day. This group must have found that the *Meiteis* had already occupied the valley of Manipur, so they settled in the hills in dispersed settlements. It is probably due to these reasons which imply a sparse nature of settlement that the Tangkhul tribe got its name. In Meitei language—literally, *Tang* means scarce and *khul* means village.[54] However, Hodson gave another version of *Tangkhul* migration. He wrote,

> "in case of the Tangkhuls, the tradition as to their origin resolves themselves into at least three groups. In the first group are the traditions which connect them with the valley and derive them thence as immigrants on account of heat and mosquitoes. According to the second group of traditions, the village of Hundung (which must be distinguished from Tangkhul Hundung) is the centre of their dispersion, and the story is clear that they sprang from immigrants from the village of Maikhel Tungam (a village which is also the traditional home of the common ancestors of the quasi-Angami tribes in the Mao group). The Tangkhul legend is to the effect that one day a sow, heavy with young, wandered from the village of Hundung and was tracked to the valley of the younger of the two brothers who had migrated from the village of Maikhel to Tungam."[55]

The *Zeliang* consisting of *Zemi* and *Liangmei* have various versions of their migrations. The descendants of *Koza* believe that they went on a hunting expedition and while pursuing a stag, lost their way home and thus settled in their present homeland.[56] But the Zeliangs themselves

54. This information has been cross examined and verified by interviewing a Tangkhul Naga, Ayo, from Manipur.
55. T.C. Hodson, *op.cit.*, pp. 8-9.
56. Based on the information from Khezhakenoma village.

say that they came through the *Japfu* mountain near *Mao* country. This view would also mean that at one time they branched out from *Khezhakenoma*. There is also an explanation of how they were termed as *Kacha Naga*. It was believed that the word was derived from the Hindustani word, *kacha* the antonym of *pukka* but the Zeliangs themselves deny this version.[57] They say that when a British officer asked the name of the tribe, an Angami interpreter said that they were all *Ketsa* meaning 'forest' in Angami because the Zeliang were known to be forest inhabitants, the land being thickly wooded.[58] Whatever may be their origin, it is erroneous on the part of the British writers to refer to them as inferior.

Another group from *Khezhakenoma* left and formed the two big villages of *Kheso* and *Sohe*. From there they moved to *Pfuchumi*, the present *Pudanamai*, then to *Pubonamai*, and onwards to *Tadubi* and so on unitl they occupied the whole of the present *Mao-Maram* country.[59] Here it is important to note the importance of *Maikhel* village of *Mao*. According to the *Khezhakenoma* legend this was the place where *Koza* stopped to rest and where he was directed by the Spirits to proceed to *Khezhakenoma*. But some *Mao* legends tell us that this village was the centre from where they migrated to other parts. Hodson wrote,

> "At Maikhel is to be seen a stone, now erect, which marks the place from which the common ancestors emerged from the earth. Maikhel is regarded as the centre from which migration took place"[60]

57. J.H. Hutton, *op.cit.*, p. 352.
58. This is the version of Zeliang group of Nagas.
59. Information of Khezhakenoma villagers.
60. T.C. Hodson, *op.cit.*, p. 13.

The group of people who left the *Mao* country first but proceeded to the area known as *Soheme,* are presently known as the *Rengmas.*[61] The present *Rengma* tribe, however, consists of a number of clans who directly migrated from *Khonoma.* Some of these clans are *Lorin, Kepen, Kemp.*[62]

The section which migrated to a distant area from *Khezhakenoma* came to be known as *Lothas*—the ones who settle in a far-off land. The *Khezha* word for *far* is *Lotha.*[63] But there are other versions too, and the *Lotha* call themselves *Kyong* probably from their own word *Kyon,* which means *Man.*[64]

The Chakhesang is a combination of three smaller tribes—*Chakri, Khezha,* and *Sangtam.* The *Khezhas* are the original descendants of *Koza* who remained in *Khezhakenoma* and the surrounding villages. The *Chakri* settled next to the *Khezha,* but further to the west. The third tribe—the *Sangtams*—is the smallest of the three and call themselves *Puchori,* again a combination of three clans—*Pu, Cho,* and *Ri.*[65] But now Puchori has become a seperate tribe and is recognised both by the Church organisation and the government.

The Angami which forms the focal point in this thesis, is also a group which traces its origins to *Khezhakenoma.* The

---

61. J.P. Mills, *op.cit.*
    J.P. Hutton, *op.cit.,* p. 35a.
62. Even in 1974 some members of these clans came to Khonoma for the clan reunion feast. The author was a participant of the feast.
63. J.P. Mills, *The Lotha Nagas, op.cit.*
64. Ben Lotha gave this information.
65. The formation of Chakhesang Tribe took place in the post Independent era and the formation of Puchori is very recent. Unfortunately there is no written record on these tribes. The only work now being done on the tribe is by N. Venuh.

legend says that a group from *Khezhakenoma* went and settled down at *Khesoura.*[66] There lived a man called *Kezieu* at *Khesoura.* He had two sons—*Pfuvio* and *Vadio. Pfuvio* stayed on and his descendants went further north, and *Vadio* migrated to *Maikhel* in *Mao* country. Vadio had four sons and two of them—*Zuonuo* and *Keyhonuo*—became the ancestors of the *Zuono-Keyhonou* group of Angamis. The descendants of *Zuono-Keyhonuo,* in the process of migration and expansion formed ten villages which later were termed by the British as the southern Angamis. These villages are *Kigwema, Viswema, Jakhama, Khuzama, Kidima, Kezoma, Phesama, Pfuchumá, Mima,* and *Mitelephe.*[67]

Our oral traditions and legends suggest that the descendants of *Zuonuo* and *Keyhonuo* increased in the village of *Kigwema* and therefore some of them decided to migrate to other villages. Hence the village acquired the name *Kigwema,* meaning 'people who occupied the old house'[68] One of these migrants known as *Vise* founded *Viswema* village. Later another group went to *Jakhama.* Some clans of *Jakhama* believe that they got their name from the word *Mejakha* which means 'to stop or block the "*Mejamia*", the northern tribes. They say that this happened because *Jakha* was sent to form a village in order to stop the northern tribes from invading the Angamis. The Angamis refer to all the northern tribes such as Semas, Lothas, Aos as *Mezhamia* or *Mejamia.* Hence, from the word *Mejakha* came Jakhama,

---

66. Shurhozelie, "Tenyidie Seminar Va Diau" in *Ura Dze,* edited by Beilieu, Kohima, 1974.
See also N.K. Das, *Agrarian Situation in India,* Delhi, 1985, Vol. I, p. 86, "The Zuonuo-Keyhonuo consider themselves as a particular clan descended from Zuonuo and Keyhonuo, the twin ancestors of all living.
67. Based on field work.
68. Literally, *Ki* = house, *gwe* = occupied or old, *ma* = man.

Kha meaning to stop or block, and *ma* meaning man[69]. Others say that one of the descendants of *Zuonuo-Keyhonuo* was a man called *Jakha*, the brother of *Vise*, who founded the village of *Jakhama*.[70] Likewise, in the process the other villages emerged due to increasing population.

It was from this group that people migrated further and formed the northern and western Angami villages. These villages were formed almost at the same time but some villages were settled before the others. In the western group *Jotsoma* and *Secuma* were settled before *Khonoma* and *Mezoma*. Likewise, Merema in the northern group was one of the oldest villages. In fact legends tell us that the present Angami religion was founded in *Merema* village. There was a man called *Jieseu* who became very rich. He wanted to give a *Feast of Merit* to his villagers but had forgotten the rituals connected with it.[71] Then he had a dream and God told him in the dream to go ahead with the preparations. *Jieseu* got ready with his *mithuns*. At night the Spirit of God came and recited all the blessings, prayers and rituals connected with the cremony. Jieseu repeated all these after Him. Thus the Angamis revived their old religious practices in course of time had been dominated by the other practices in the process of their long migration.[72]

Natural circumstances caused them to further migrate and in due course the northern villages of *Kohima, Nerhema, Tophe, Keruma, Merema, Rukhroma, Ciedema, Seiyhama,*

---

69. Vithuto an Angami from the Jakhama village gave this information.
70. *Ibid.*
71. A Feast of Merit is a symbol of status. The greater the number of such feasts given to the village, the higher one's social standing. Thus, there are degrees of Feasts of Merit. Petenihu Chase of Merhu of Khonoma village was kind enough to narrate all the details of the legend of Jiesieu to the writer.
72. *Ibid.*

Chieziema, Phekerukrilma, Chiephobozhu, Gariphe, Tsiese, Vipho, Diho, Jumetu and *Chiechama* were formed.[73] In the western sector, the villages of *Jotsoma* and *Secuma* prospered and grew and soon the other villages of *Khonoma, Mezoma, Kiruphema, Menguzhuma, Thekrujunama* and *Dzulekema* were formed.[74]

The last group of villages that were formed were known as *Chakhroma*, literally meaning 'those who live below the road'. They were so referred to because they went down to the plains for settlement as a result of Angami expansion. It was this group that first came into contact with the *Dimasas* in Dimapur, as one of the main villages, *Chumukedima*, was settled on the plains near *Dimapur* the capital of the *Dimasa* kingdom.[75] The *Chakhroma* villages too began to expand and in the process formed the new villages of *Piphema, Medziphema, Sithekiema, Ruziephema, Socunoma, Pherima, Tsiepama* and *Tsuuma, Siethima.*[76]

The Nagas who branched out of *Khezhakenoma*, broadly speaking, split up into two groups. The six tribes of *Chakhesang, Angami, Rengma, Mao, Maram* and *Zeliang* termed themselves as *Tenyimia* and more or less functioned in a confederation.[77] At this stage we have no means of knowing when the *Tenyimia* group was formed, but we do know that the *Tenyimia* group is divided into two maieteis

73. Of all these villages it is Kohima which had figured prominently in records from the British occupation of Naga Hills and after. However, the importance of other villages in their own context is no less significant.
74. Based on field work.
75. Dimasas are among the earliest settlers in Assam valley. The capital of Dimasas was in Dimapur when they ruled Assam in ancient times. R.M. Nath, *The Background of Assamese Culture*, Shillong, 1949, p. 72.
76. These villages are presently located in western portions of Naga Hills.
77. From the field work conducted by the scholar.

known as Thepa and Thevo. Legend says that Thepa and Thevo were brothers and all the *Tenyimia* are believed to be descendants of these two brothers.

The Tenyimia called all the other tribes as Mezhamia which is a rather derogatory term. The *Tenyimia* group shares some common traditions, culture and agricultural practices such as terrace cultivation whereas the *Mezhamia* group practice jhum cultivation and were usually naked or semi-naked. Some traditions say that the *Tenyimia* are descendants of *Tenyiu*,[78] Others say that it comes from the word *Tanyumia* meaning 'those who ran away' because they left their original homeland and migrated elsewhere.[79]

The Angamis seem to have emerged prosperous and powerful because they controlled the general affairs of some of the tribes for centuries.[80] One of the reasons for the Angamis becoming powerful enough to manage the affairs of the other tribes is that in the processs of breaking up, the Angamis took up settled agriculture and settled in areas which were more suitable for good agriculture and thereby improved their means of subsistence and increased their production. Hunting was left as a supplement. Gradually their number increased and they subdued the neighbouring tribes.

It would not be historically incorrect to say that the Angamis laid the foundation of the process of state formation. We refer to it here as 'state formation' although under the Angamis the state did not develop to the extent of completely transforming tribal organization but the symptoms of the dominating process of production did emerge with them. The most important factor that emerged

78. Shurhozalie, *op.cit.*
79. Zievilie Sakhrie of Khonoma village gave this information.
80. The Zeliangs and the Liangmeis especially were dominated by the Angamis.

is that the Angamis demanded tribute from other tribes as already mentioned and provided security to them in return.[81] These were the basic fundamentals of the Angami state. It appears that as part of their tribal organization, the Angamis did not interfere with the internal affairs of the other tribes, but continued to remain satisfied with the collection of tribute.[82]

The refusal to pay tribute was taken as a denouncement of Angami power and authority. Such villages were burnt and properties were confiscated. A series of such developements gave the Angamis a political strength and security. It was from this time onwards that we find that the Angamis remained in constant touch with the affairs of the tribes bordering their territory.[83]

However, in spite of all these advantages, the Angamis never formed a state as defined by H.J.M. Claessen.[84] Curiously enough, the population of the Angamis, like that of all the Nagas, began to decrease when the British arrived in their land. This strange phenomenon occurred due to many factors which is beyond the scope of this thesis at present. But the British themselves recorded as Hodson wrote,

> "There is, however, enough evidence to show that the Naga population is slowly diminishing. A village like Maram had 900 houses in 1859, 200 houses in 1891, 120 in 1900. There is, therefore, less pressure of population on land and formation of colonies is for the moment checked."[85]

---

81. J.H. Hutton, *op.cit.*, p. 352.
82. *Ibid.*
    Tribute was given in the form of woven cloths, spears, grain etc.
83. Laxmi Devi, *Ahom-Tribal Relations*, Gauhati, 1968.
84. H.J.M. Claessen and Peter Skalnick, *op.cit.*
85. T.C. Hodson, *op.cit.*, p. 19.

This factor was one of the main reasons that checked the expansion and development of Angami economy and political power.[86]

The Dimasa who were the earliest settlers of the region came into contact with the Angamis. But since the Angamis were expanding their territory to the plains, there was necessarily a lack of cordial relations between the two. The Angamis fought and defeated the remaining Dimasas and seized their capital at Dimapur which still forms part of present Nagaland.[87] The relationship soon took on the nature of intermittent periods of war and peace, and both were influenced by each other's military tactics and other affairs as well. In cultural and social spheres we find various cases of intermarriage between the Dimasas and the Angamis right down to the present day.[88] Hutton wrote of the Angami relationship with the Dimasa Kacharis follows:

> "They must have come into contact with the Kacharis, whose capital was at Dimapur on the edge of Angami country, and legends of the Kachari king Bhim are still current among the Kacha Nagas and the Angamis of

---

86. The decrease of the native population wherever colonization took place was a common phenomenon such as in the case of Aborigines of Australia, Maoris of New Zealand and the indigenous people of America. In Naga Hills too the population began to diminish in the 19th century. There could be many reasons for this. A sudden contact with western civilization brought new diseases. In other cases, due to native resistance of colonial power, large numbers were decimated when villages were burnt, crops destroyed and the remaining population dispersed.
87. Prior to the attack of Angamis on Dimasas, the Ahoms had sacked the Dimasa Capital at Dimapur and defeated Dimasas.
    F.A. Gait, op. cit., p. 97. For details see R.L. Hangloo, *Situating Medieval Indian State* (Ed.) Delhi-1995, pp. 71-119.
88. The Pfulise clan of Khonoma are the descendants of a Dimasa princess who married a man from the Meyase clan called Pfulise. Information collected from Theyievizo of Meyase clan of Khonoma village.

> Khonoma.... there is also a legend current among the Kacharis of Diger Mauza below Henima that when Bhim Raja built his great Keddah at Sonapur, in that Mauza, he fell in love with a Nagini whom he found in the jungle and who became by him the ancestress of the Diger Kacharis, who pride themselves on their descent."[89]

With the Manipuris the attitude of the Angamis was very much the same as with the Dimasa. There were wars at times but the Manipuris generally adopted a friendly relationship with the Angamis most of the time. The Manipuris occasionally invaded Angamis in retaliation to the Angami raids on the Manipuri subjects. Much later, after the Angami settlement, Hutton recorded one such ugly incident.

> "With the Manipuris the relations of the Angamis, at any rate, were anything but friendly, as somewhere about 1833 a Manipuri raid was made into Angami country as far as Kohima, which the Manipuris attacked and burnt, slaughtering a large number of the inhabitants."[90]

Angamis also carried out trade and commerce with Manipuris from ancient times. This friendly relationship proved advantageous to the Angamis. They learnt the art of gun-making and gun-powder and other artisanal skills from the Manipuris. Even in the matter of defence, we have references prove that the Angamis used to hire the services of Manipuris to invade the other tribes.[91]

Though the Ahoms came much later, their contact with the Nagas is worth mentioning. In fact, the Ahoms entered Assam in the 13th century A.D. through the Naga Hills with

---

89. J.H. Hutton, *op.cit.*, p. 13.
90. *Ibid.*, p. 13-14.
91. Recorded from Theyievizo of Merhu clan, Khonoma.

their leader, Sukhapa.[92] Of 'all the people, the Nagas strongly resisted but were given severe treatment by Sukhapa's men.[93] For quite some time the hostile feelings continued but in the past centuries, we find the Nagas and the Ahoms living in a friendly manner. Perhaps the Nagas had realised that the areas occupied by the Ahoms were the main outlet to the rest of the sub-continent of India.

Before we close this chapter, it may be observed that the whole Naga society was divided into various tribes and each tribe was independent of the other. There was no centralized political structure and each tribe was governed by its own chiefs or elders under various custom and traditions.[94] The transition from primitive settlement to a more developed type of village settlement was, of course, accompanied by the pressure of increasing population, the search for subsistence, the struggle and aspirations for improved material conditions. Having these factors as the basic objective, there were a series of efforts made by the Angamis before the establishment of *Khonoma* and *Kohima* as permanent seats of their social and economic life. The series of efforts carried out by the Angamis included clan alliances, development of terrace cultivation, improvement of implements and other challenges imposed by demography and environment before they finally choose to settle down in the present village.

---

92. P. Gogoi, *op.cit.*, p. 251-252.
93. E.A. Gait, *op.cit.*, pp. 78-79.
94. There are about 34 Naga tribes. Sixteen in Nagaland itself, ten in Manipur, and some in Burma, Assam and Arunachal Pradesh. Each of these tribes have indigenous social organization of their own, *e.g.*, among the Konyaks the absolute power rests with the chiefs. The Angami, Ao, Mao and Tangkhul have a kind of democratic system run by the village elders, likewise the Sema have their own system with some variations.

3

KOHIMA

After a long drawn process of migration and settlement, the important centres which emerged in the Angami country are Kohima and Khonoma. In this chapter we shall be focusing on Kohima. Kohima is said to be the second largest populated village in the world and the biggest village in Asia in terms of population.[1]

One of the oldest legends still surviving in the minds of the villagers is that this area was first discovered and chosen for settlement by a man called *Whio* and that Kohima in course of time came to be termed as *Kewhimia*, named after *Whio*, which means 'men of Whio'.[2]

The other version of the origin of this village is that the first settlers were *Usou* and *Rhieo* who came with their sister *Mesei-u* and her son *Tsiera* from *Kigwema*.[3] These people saw from afar a huge tree on a hillock on the land where Kohima now stands. The tree appeared to be in the centre of the area, and they searched for seven days to locate it.

1. Kohima is presently the capital of the hill state of Nagaland.
2. There is a section who attribute the origin of Kohima to this legend. Shurhozelie (50) of Kohima told the scholar this legend.
3. Salhouthie (70) of Kohima told this folk tale to the scholar.

When eventually they found the tree they came down to settle in Kohima. The legend also reads that the first settlers had a dream where they saw plenty of white and black ants mixing. This dream was interpreted to mean that this place was a land where the population would increase and that strangers would come and settle here. Notwithstanding the dream, it becomes very clear that a group of the early settlers did realize that Kohima was a place which would assume a central character and welcome people from various directions. This is strongly supported by the fact that in the Angami language "Mia bu u Kehi kepfu-u chutuo" means "we shall welcome people" or "people shall come to us". The name *Kewhimia* was adopted by the British as Kohima, and was eventually accepted by the Nagas thereafter.[4]

Tradition shows that the early settlers found Kohima to be a land of seven lakes and seven hills.[5] Later, Kohima developed into a village with seven gates. Curiously enough it is to be noted that from earliest times the number seven has figured prominently in its history and tradition. Seven is a mysterious and sacred number for the Angami. Much of the folklore is connected with the number seven, such as seven days, seven years, seven clans, and so on. For instance, even to the present day, the fine for theft is fixed at seven times the value stolen. The reference to the seven lakes is a clear indication of the fact that the land had a good water source to start terrace cultivation which was very important to the early settlers for permanent occupation of the place.

---

4. Visietuo Linyu narrated the history of the first settlers of Kohima to the scholar.
5. Shurhozelie, *A Ra Kezevi*, Kohima, 1984, p 2.
The original word used here denotes 'lakes'. But from all geographical information, the existence of lakes in this area is highly unlikely. The reference must, therefore, have been to springs or ponds.

Kohima, from ages past, continues to be in the heart of the Angami country and is surrounded by eleven villages: *Jotsoma, Rukhroma, Secuma, Ciedema, Mima, Merema, Chieziema, Nerhema, Phesama, Pfuchama* and *Chakhaba*. The traditional village has a population of more than twenty thousand and the capital city which has grown around Kohima village has a population of around one lakh. Kohima, the capital of Nagaland, has grown out of the original Kohima village. The original village still stands with its own tribal social organization. Since in the early process of settlement and evolution of various Angami villages we do not find any evidence of both the village of Kohima and Khonoma, it becomes all the more important to probe thoroughly and establish the various factors that led to the evolution of these villages.

We have seen how over a period of time more fertile land and the subsequent growth of population, and search for sustenance split the early Naga tribes into various settlements of *Semas, Lothas, Rengmas, Mao, Maram, Tangkhul, Zeliang, Chakhesang,* and so on. After these processes of splitting up into various tribes took place, each tribe fixed its own perimeter for carrying out their struggle for sustenance with communal labour. Each tribe developed its tribal or clan social and economic organization under the supreme authority of their chiefs or elders. But in course of time each tribe aspired for maximum land, forests, pasture and it became necessary to push back each others borders. This phenomenon being strongly supported by the gradual growth of population, introduced in-fighting among various tribes which had branched out from the same root.

In due course some of the weaker and smaller tribes carried out a defence against others by intra-tribal alliances. In this intra-tribal welfare, we find that the Angamis emerged powerful due to some important historical reasons. It was at this stage that the early foundations of material culture were being laid down. The first and foremost reason for their emergence as a dominant tribe was the geographical character of the territory they occupied. When we look at these settlements we find that the Angami settlements were well connected with the region of Assam on one side and Manipur on the other.[6] The history of Assam reveals that the process of agrarian organization had started much earlier with comparatively developed farming and agricultural technology. Besides, Assam was easily linked with India. So penetration of any influence into Assam was part of the usual historical process. The area bordering Manipur was also occupied by the Angamis or by related tribes and, like Assam, they continued to be influenced by the developing technology in agriculture, craft-making and other fields.[7] It appears that the situation proved to be an added asset to the Angamis because they were the first to receive the waves of development from the outside world through these two directions.[8] As Assam and Manipur were the two states with advanced culture, economy and politics from ancient times.

The other important factor that helped in imposing their dominance was the environment they were in. When the process of settling down was taking place, they chose to

---

6. B.C. Allen, *Assam District Gazetteers*, Shillong, 1905.
   T.C. Hodson, *op.cit.*
   M. Horam, *op.cit.*, pp. 5-7, 42, 43.
7. Lakshmi Debi, *op.cit.*
8. Assam and Manipur were the states with advanced culture, economy and politics from ancient times.
   S.K. Bhuyan, *Studies in the History of Assam*, Gauhati, 1965, pp. 1-77.
   S.K. Chatterjee, *The Place of Assam in the History and Civilization of India*, Gauhati, 1955.
   K.L. Barua, *Early History of Kamarupa*, Gauhati, 1966, pp. 96-103.

settle in an area which was endowed with rich forests, pastures, flora, fauna, springs and streams which continued to irrigate their lands for terrace cultivation almost throughout the year. Naturally, a clan endowed with all the possibilities for their hunting exercises and some amount of land for settled agriculture to supplement their hunting increased in number and posed their authority over smaller and relatively poorer clans over a period of time.[9] Another factor that proved the growth of the Angamis as a powerful tribe was the support provided by the *Tenyimia* group. In the earlier chapter we have illustrated how the Angamis evolved out of *Tenyimia* as a seperate tribe. We find that given the above mentioned advantages, the *Tenyimia* tribes settled in the immediate neighbourhood of the Angamis. They gave all support to the rising Angamis and always provided defence from other tribes. These are some of the factors which favoured the emergence of the Angamis as a prominent tribe in the Naga hills. In fact, we do not have any literary or even oral evidence for the earlier period but it appears that there must have been mutual assistance between rulers of Manipur, Assam and the Angamis.[10] It was these factors which appear to have favoured the emergence of the Angamis as a powerful group able to subject other tribes and levy tribute from them.

Before we proceed further, it becomes historically essential to probe the emergence of Kohima into an

9. David Laibman in his thesis regarding modes of production has brought out the analysis of this aspect clearly wherein he also stresses the accumulation of surplus as a necessary though not sufficient condition for evolution of the preliminaries of class antagonism in the tribal formation. D Laibman, "Modes of Production and Theories of Transition" in *Science and Society*, Vol. XLVIII, No. 3, Fall, 1984, New York, pp. 268-269.
10. Milada Ganguli, *A Pilgrimage to the Nagas*, Delhi 1984, pp. 1-15.

important Angami centre. Why did the Kohima settlement of the Angamis emerge so important? What are the various factors responsible for its development? For explaining this development we have no other alternative but to examine the emergence of various clans which led to the formation of Kohima the intra-clan alliances, feuds and mergers of those various social and material processes which linked and de-linked these various clans together. Earlier in this chapter we have demonstrated how Kohima was selected by some of its first settlers because of its resources and how they perceived that this place would welcome and accommodate more people in course of time.

Let us first look into the history of this clan formation as told by the Kohima folk themselves.[11]

LHISEMIA — As mentioned earlier, the first settlers in Kohima were two brothers—*Usou* and *Rhieo.*[12] These two brothers lived together in harmony. But one day, *Rhieo's* hunting dog killed his brother *Usou's* child. The ancient Angami customary law known as *themu* required that *Rhieo* be exiled from the village as the consequence of this, and accordingly *Rhieo* made preparations to do so. His grief stricken brother, *Usou,* begged him to stay and not leave him bereft of both child and brother. But *Rhieo,* in keeping with the ancient law, left the village and settled at a nearby place called *Mouthuzhu* which falls in the present *Lhiesemia* area. He had five sons, three of whom—*Soukhrie,* Linyu, and *Khielie* formed *Rhiepfumia* clan which was named after *Rhieo.*

When *Rhieo* and *Usou* came to Kohima, they were accompanied by their sister, *Mesei-u,* and her son *Tsiera. Tsiera* became a successful man and it is said that he and his

---

11. See Table on Clan Organization at the end of this Chapter.
12. Salhouthie (70) of Kohima village related to the history of *Lhisemia* clan.

mother were the first Kohima settlers to have performed the Feast of Merit. *Tsiera* had five sons—*Mepfuo, Tsikha, Vizonuo, Yhome* and *Dzuvichu*—whose descendants multiplied and formed the *Tsieramia* clan.

Another clan that emerged was *Huoruotso, Houruo* who came from the *Zeliang* country was adopted into the village.[13] In those days, it was a common practice to adopt a child from another village or even another tribe. Such was the case of *Huoruo*. Although the story of his adoption forms an interesting snippet of Angami folklore, it is not pertinent to our analysis at this stage. What is important is that *Huoruo* prospered and became the father of *Huoruotsu* clan through his sons *Suorhie, Liezie, Rulho* and *Kesiezie*. Thus we had the three small clans of *Rhiepfumia, Tsieramia,* and *Huoruotsu*. However, each of these clans was too weak to stand up to the fighting of other clans alone. It was at such a critical stage of confrontation that a man from the *Mao* tribe came to settle in Kohima. It was this man who united these three clans by performing a small feast which involved the killing of a pig—a tribal delicacy at that time.[14] The merger gave birth to a new clan called *Lhisemia,* literally meaning 'three clans'. Thus, this clan which was now the biggest and most powerful was formed not by the descendants of one man, as is usually the case, but was a banding together of three different clans and has worked with amazing solidarity.

---

13. Duorhilie (80) of Kohima village narrated the history of *Huoruotsu* clan to the scholar. Huoro came from *Kenoma* village, and his clan there is known as *Tolotsu*.
14. Salhouthie, *op.cit*.
The name of the Mao man who united these clans was *Krenyi* who adopted the name *Krunyu* when he came to Kohima.
Vikrulie Belho of Kohima village provided this information.

DAPFU — When *Rhieo* left the original Kohima site, he left behind two of his sons—*Yiese* and *Sachu*. These two sons also banded together with a certain man called *Dapfu* who was also an immigrant from the Mao tribe.[15] The clan thus formed was called *Dapfutsu*, taking of *Dapfu*'s name because he was the oldest member of the alliance. This clan is divided into five sub-clans-three of which *Khezie*, *Kire*, and *Keretsu*—are descended from Dapfu. The other two still bear the names of *Yiese* and *Sachu*. These clans are occupying the original site of Kohima. The ancient seat is still contained by this clan. Another sub-clan of Dapfu is Keditsu who merged into the clan at a later stage.

PFUCHA — The third major clan called *Pfuchatsu* was named after *Pfucha* who was one of the descendants of *Usou*, brother of *Rhieo*.[16] *Pfucha*'s father died when he was a baby and his mother remarried a man from *Chumukedima* and settled there with *Pfucha*. He grew up to be popular and sociable in the village. This stirred feelings of jealousy in the hearts of some of his friends who began taunting him, saying that he was an outsider who did not belong to *Chukedima*. Puzzled, he asked his mother the meaning of the taunt, but she refused to tell him, until one day, he confronted his mother alone in the house, and forced her to reveal the truth. She unfolded to him the story of his origin and seeing her son's desire to return to his *true* father's people, sent word to Kohima asking that some men be sent to escort to him back. When two of *Usuo*'s men arrived. *Pfucha* left *Chumukedima* with his mother's blessing. She gave him one servant, some cattle and also promised that all the lands on which his cattle stopped to rest the night would belong to him. Thus he

---

15. The direction of Angami migration took place from the Mao country, following the general trend at that time.
16. Ado Rutsa (60) of Kohima village narrated this.

gained land large enough to house a settlement. In course of time he grew to be a man of influence and stature, so much so, that the descendants of *Usuo* merged with him, forming the sub-clause of *Usuo, Kerutsa, Sote, Rame, Keyho* and *Pienyu* under the banner of *Pfucha* clan.

TSUTUO—This clan was the result of a chance meeting between a man from the *Semoma* clan of Khonoma and a girl of Kohima from *Pfucha*'s clan. One day, as the man was travelling, he stopped to have his lunch in this girl's field. The outcome of this brief encounter was that the girl soon became heavy with child. In course of time, she secretly gave birth to her child and carried the new-born baby to the village. When accosted and asked what it was that she was carrying, she replied that it was a *Tsutuo,* which means 'cucumber' in Angami. Thus the boy came to be called *Tsutuo.* He grew up in Kohima and had five sons—*Sekhose, Belho, Solo, Whuorie* and *Geisuo.* Their descendants multiplied and formed the *Tsutuonomia* clan.[17]

From this discussion on the formation of various clans in Kohima, it becomes amply clear that initially when the process of settling took place the split from *Khezhakenoma* had left a small number in each clan. Though from the resource point of view, the Angamis were endowed with all advantages, their small number was their constant drawback. Besides, there was a regular threat from Manipur and Assam which were bordering the Angami territory.[18] It was as a result of this that we find that the

---

17. Satuo (60) of Kohima village told the history of *Tsutuonomia* clan to the scholar.
18. Although the relations between the Angamis and neighbouring Assam and Manipur were generally good, occasional border disputes did occur.
    Robert Reid, *History of Frontier Areas Bordering Assam*, Delhi, 1942, pp. 99-125.

Angamis of Kohima were looking for more people to settle there. Tradition provides evidence that people were also sometimes brought and adopted from other villages and tribes.[19] It also appears that the intra-clan fighting forced these clans to accommodate people from outside. Here it is interesting to observe that this intra-clan fighting was generated by various factors. The early tribal settlers had not given up their primitive nature such as the forcible capturing of each other's territory, taking men as captives and hotheadedness which sometimes led to serious consequences. We have many examples of this nature which also blocked the upward economic development of these clans. The feuds over hunting domain or even some of the various arguments on festive and other occasions gave birth to intra-clan warfare which persisted with the tribal mode of life for a long time. As we have already illustrated, it was as a result of these early clan feuds that *Huoruotsu*, *Rhiepfu* and *Tsiera* clans merged into a big clan known as *Lhisemia* to consolidate their strength. In fact, there were many more such alliances which led to the formation of other such clans, but we are unfortunate in not possessing all the details at present.

Generally the increasing insecurity created by this intra-clan warfare continued for a long time in the history of the Angami villages, and Kohima was no exception. It seems that due to this insecurity, the various clans were forced into alliances and alignments and in this process, we find some villages emerging more powerful. This intra-clan fighting was very closely connected with mutual raids.

When Kohima started emerging as a powerful village, we find *Keruma* also growing along the same lines.

---

19. The present *Theunuomia* clan of Kohima is an example of such an adoption.

We have evidence to suggest that in the early period, the people of Kohima raided their neighbouring villages. (Evidence of this was gleaned from the fabric of common knowledge and even today, the smaller villages around Kohima remain bitter at the onslaughts suffered in the past.) There can be two reasons for this either the population of Kohima increased as mentioned above and their hunting and other resources did not increase in response to the growing population, and their only alternative was to look to the resources of the neighbouring villages and capture men and materials; or, the other possibility can be that since the population was less in Kohima and they had large measures of land available, they would forcibly capture the neighbours in order to secure labour power. This reason sounds more plausible, because keeping in view the nature of the land and the living conditions, the population must have always remained limited.

When Kohima started emerging as a powerful village, we find Keruma also growing the same lines.[20] This became further cause for trouble. Kohima people wanted to plunder and destroy *Keruma*, but could not do so because *Keruma* under the legendary warrior, *Razieo*, was too powerful.[21] After trying every means at their disposal, the people of Kohima could not succeed in destroying *Razieo*. But an account of the story which survives even today bears a remarkable similarity to the story of Samson and Delilah

20. The old Keruma village was settled in what is now Kohima Raj Bhavan and Officer's Hill. When Keruma was defeated, they left their village and settled in their present site, but retained the name of their old village.
21. Satuo Kuotsu (60) of Kohima village told the legend of *Razieo*.

related in the Bible as recorded is the Book of Judges. The people of Kohima sent their most beautiful girl to the field which bordered *Keruma* village with intent to tempt *Razieo*. He fell in love with the girl and ultimately married her. The people of Kohima tried to find the secret of *Rezieo*'s weakness and they found out through his wife that it was on sacred days when performing rituals that he would not put on armour and was ill-equipped and vulnerable. It was on one such occasion when his beloved signalled her clansmen by spreading a white shawl outside her house which could be seen from Kohima, that they attacked *Keruma*. It was thus that *Rezieo* was caught unawares due to his trust of the traitor woman. He was killed in the encounter. After *Razieo*'s death, *Keruma* was besieged for several months. When the planting season came, the people of *Keruma* had no other choice but to leave the old village and migrate to another area, which forms the present *Keruma* village. In this way, the people of Kohima occupied what is the whole of the old *Keruma* land and later emerged as an important Angami centre. The old Keruma village was in what is now Kohima Raj Bhavan and Officer's Hill. When Keruma was defeated they left their village and settled in the present village but retained the name of the old village

When we look at the nature of technology that Kohima made use of, we find that it was not of an advanced type but was very much primitive in nature because of the isolation from the rest of the world. But their tools certainly had their own peculiarities. The people had their own technological devices for carrying out agriculture, hunting, weaving, spinning, transportation, tools for the manufacture, of baskets, brewing, lighting, ornamentation and designing of fighting equipment. The number of agricultural implements remained limited since the Angamis in general depended mainly on hunting as well as jhuming and terrace cultivation for their livelihood.[22]

The hoe was used for digging the soil in the jhum and terrace processes. A long wooden hammer was used for breaking the earthern clods. A bamboo rake was used for threshing the paddy, and for husking the paddy a wooden mortar and pestle was used. In agriculture, apart from rice, the other crops were corn, millets, job's tear, soyabeans etc. for which the same implements were used. For clearing the jungle and cutting down the plants and trees the Angami used the dao.[23] Iron was a speciality in the technological device before the Angamis settled at Kohima. A sickle was used for cutting the paddy sheaves at harvest time. A rake made of bamboo sticks with a wooden handle was used for clearing weeds.

Apart from cultivation, hunting was an equally important source of subsistence. In the early days hunting may often have taken precedence over agriculture especially when the forests and terrain were more abundant in wild life and posed difficulties for jhuming. For hunting there were various categories of spears with iron tips at both ends. The variation in size of these spears depended on the suitability of the occasion and the kind of hunt. The spear was also used by the warriors and was often beautifully decorated and designed. The length of the spears varied from four to six feet. They were, however, incomplete as a weapon without the shield which was made out of bear, elephant and tiger hides. The shield was about four to five feet long and approximately three feet

---

22. This evidence has been collected from the field work carried out by the author.
23. *Ibid.* The dao is the most important implement among all the Naga tribes. There is a little variation is its design and size, however, from tribe to tribe.

wide. These shields were often decorated with feathers along the edges, each feather signifying various achievements in war and social life. The dao, which has a multi-technological purpose, was used for hunting. It was also used in man to man combat and was specifically useful in cutting off the heads of enemies. In appearance it resembles a thick, short sword. But unlike a sword, its tip is squared off and not tapered. It varies in length from one to four feet. Another weapon used was the bow and arrow. Like the dao and spear, it varied in size and in the process of handling and was used during the *Sekrenyi* festival.[24] It was different, however, from the type used by other Naga tribes. Although firearms or muskets were introduced to the Angamis by the Manipuris in the medieval period, it was only when the British that the Angamis became familiar with more sophisticated tools of weaponary.[25]

Since the climate of the area was of a moderate type, the Angamis depended only on cotton to protect their bodies. Every family used to spin their own clothes. The climate dictated their choice of cotton as a crop and did not necessitate the practice of stock grazing for wool. Sheep and goats were raised and kept for meat instead. It is also probable that the use of wool, needing a more developed technological apparatus, was not adopted since cotton, simpler to process and weave, served their needs equally well. Weaving of cotton was carried out on a wooden frame and loin loom. A wooden machine was also used for the

---

24. On such occasions, a Wooden effigy is constructed and the men of the village shoot at this effigy. This was done to commemorate the rituals of hunting and of war.
25. The various items of weaponary exposed to them by the British included mountain guns, rifles, cannons and so on.
    Alexander Mackenzie, *A History of the Relations of the Government with the Hill Tribes of the North East Frontier of Bengal*, Calcutta, 1884.

processing of cotton balls into yarns. The whole process of the manufacture of cotton cloths from start to finish was the sole work of women.

Before the Angamis developed proper villages like Kohima and Khonoma, there does not seem to have existed trade or commerce with neighbouring states which should have involved various mechanisms for transporting goods from one area to another. Besides this, the Angami were not dependant on those domestic and other items which would have to be procured from outside. It will not be wrong to state that the growth of villages and the expansion of Angami areas to the plains broke the self-sufficiency of the Angami and increased their dependance on outside elements. It is as a result of this that we find the technology of transport almost absent in the pre-Kohima phase. For collecting and carrying purposes they used cane containers and baskets. In some rare instances, the Angami reared horses but they themselves do not seem to have used them for transport and instead used them for bartering and sale. There is a mention of the horse in Angami folklore, but this animal does not appear to have played any vital or significant role in their daily life. It was considered more as a mysterious animal, and the Angami would not eat horse meat.

Some small iron implements were used for making cane baskets, containers, wood carvings and for the construction of houses and bridges. Use of bamboo and cane were indispensable. In fact, bamboo formed an important and integral part of the tribal life. It was used not only for raising structures, fencing, implements, warfare, lighting system and in making other articles for decoration, but even as a food in the form of bamboo shoots. Bamboo is such an indispensable item in the whole of South East Asia that one can even use the term 'Bamboo Culture' in relation to this area. Like other societies which are technologically backward, the lighting arrangements mostly consisted of burning resinated pine, dry bamboo and firewood. In most cases, wooden logs were burnt for cooking, and for heat as well as for lighting purposes.

Apart from all these items there were intricate objects which were used for entertainment. Such items were the musical instruments and ornaments. These items did not assume significance because of their entertainment value alone, but they had deep roots in the religious and tribal culture. For example, blowing the buffalo horn was not only reserved for festive occasions but was a traditional means of calling people on various occasions. The flute and a sort of Jewish harp, a one-stringed violin, a single stringed instrument called *tati* played on the fingers were used by the Angamis. All these instruments are still in current use among the Angami villagers although their use is gradually dying out.

The brewing of local rice beer (*zu*) has been practised by most of the Naga societies since early times. It was taken as an essential part of their daily diet and also used as a means of expressing joy and merry-making on festive occasions. Rice beer was also used for ritualistic and religious purposes. Rice beer symbolically signifies strength and life and its inclusion in rituals and prayers forms an essential part of religious and social practices, being held in great esteem and reverence. For instance, at the time of birth, rice beer is put first to the baby's lips before any other food. It is also used to warm the spirit in meeting halls and councils.

In a society where the materialistic culture had not penetrated to large degree in the early period, the sense of making and wearing ornaments is an important and interesting field of study. Looking to their past, they seem to have travelled a long way from their original homeland. Whatever the origin of the ornaments at that stage, they went on assimilating whatever seemed to them beautiful and fitting to their customs. The more common ornaments that Angamis used to wear were earrings, necklaces, headgear, beads, ivory armlets, cane leggings, and a kilt decorated with cowrie shells. Gradually, their contact with the neighbouring tribes of Assam and other non-tribals added many more items to their ornamentation from time to time. The introduction of silver and coins in ornamentations was a nineteenth century development, when the increasing penetration of money economy took place.

Angami tools and technology were thus primitive in nature. The chief bottleneck in development was due primarily to the isolation that they maintained with the rest of the world. But it was historically impossible to continue in isolation. This was made all the more apparent with events such as the appearance of British colonization on the North Eastern scene. The effects of this colonization will be discussed further in the next chapter.

From ancient times down to the colonial period, the Angami centre of Kohima has a long history which poses some important questions:

(*a*) How could this centre survive and remain uninfluenced by the expanding Brahmanization process which had enveloped the whole of Assam and even portions of Manipur?

(*b*) How Buddhism which went to South East Asia from this region remain uninfluenced.

(*c*) What was the nature of the strength which kept the Angamis in possession of this centre as their political social and economic seat?

In suggesting a solution, we have got to understand the motives behind Brahmanization or Sanskritization. From the time of its conception, the process of Sankritization was an ideological instrument used by ancient and early medieval rulers of India in expanding their area of influence.[26] In Assam as well, this movement had similar aims. But the environment was not quite conducive because in Assam there were several tribes.[27] Apart from that, a problem was also posed by the migration of the *Ahoms* into Assam. Still, in the ancient period there were reference to prove that some of the Assamese Brahmins did attempt the Sanskritization of Nagas but could not succeed. Some old Angamis would refer to priests as '*Bramuno*' which is a clear cut indication.[28] However, on the other hand, the process must not have registered much progress due to the problem of internal consolidation. Secondly, the ruler of Assam might not have given much encouragement because this expansion of Sanskritization would not bring any revenue from Naga Hills. As the Naga Hills were endowed with meagre resources and not much land was available to support the establishment of Brahmanical design. The other important reason which did not permit the Brahmin influence to grow was that, compared to the sanskritized tribes of the *Boros, Ahoms,* and *Manipuris,* the Angamis were not prepared to sacrifice their communal indigenous organization to a stratified *varna* and later to a caste heirarchy. This becomes clear from the fact that even after getting Christianized, the Angamis have not severed their connection with their tribal heritage. The Angamis were

26. The best illustration of this nature is provided by the *Boros, Manipuris, Ahoms* and *Dimasas* who got Hinduised and witnessed an intense stratification on caste lines.
J.B. Bhattacharjee, *op.cit.*, pp. 6-8.
27. In Assam also, in the pre-Ahom times, the process of Brahmanization dissolved the tribal structure. In the Ahom period, conversion was taken over by Shankar Devas'neo-Vaishnavism.
S.N. Sharma, *The Neo-Vaishnavaite Movement and the Satra Institution of Assam*, Gauhati, 1966.
28. Thepfuwhetuo (60) of Khonoma gave this information.

also aware of the fact that when the neighbouring tribes were assimilated into the Brahmanical system, they were delegated to the ranks of the lower castes, whereas as tribals operating within their own traditional organizational structure, the Angamis would remain as free and as equal as any man created by God. The influence of the neighbouring regions have left a deep imprint on the Angami society. They would not allow any change which would stratify them on exploitative lines by non-Nagas. However, one cannot be sure about the survival of such feelings with the growing penetration of money economy.

In an environment where agrarian economy was not predominant and people had to depend on hunting and other means of subsistence, it was the indigenous social organization which could help them because hunting or even for that matter terrace cultivation could not be carried without communal labour. It was a practice among the Angamis both in hunting and in terrace cultivation that communal effort was utilized in order to effect the maximum benefit and efficiency in the practice of these tasks. The system of communal labour was on an organized level, called *peli* where a group of young people would work in each others' fields in rotation. Sometimes the whole village would also join together in certain prescribed tasks known as *Mechutho*.

Whereas the *varna* orientation did not permit the mixing of two *varnas* even in a single religion. Besides religion, the Angamis with their early Mongoloid traditions and customs had a completely distinct way of life from the rest of Assam. All this evidence suggests that the Angamis remained apart particularly in the religio-cultural aspects. Politically and economically there was mutual exchange in various respects. Buddhism for some strange historical incidence, Buddhism never touched the Nagas, although Buddhist influence reached the very edge of Naga hills.

We find that Kohima was more easily accessible and gradually got transformed into an urban centre within the tribal mode. It was from here that the people from the interior would come and get their products exchanged and gain awareness about the new influences of technology and economy. This development seems to have played a vital role in transforming Kohima from a tribal village into a centre of Angami civilization. It is the urban nature of Kohima which increased the mobility within Naga society.

From the establishment of *Ahom* rule, we get a lot of evidence to prove that there was regular contact between the Angamis and the plains of Assam. In fact many Angami chiefs were rewarded with gifts by *Ahom* rulers and there commenced a good relationship of trade and commerce-

> "The Naga tribes bordering the plains were in constant communication with the plains for trade purposes during Ahom rule. They carried on trade in their hill products like cotton, betel leaves (pan), ginger, taro (kachchu), and salt and in exchange carried back articles in which their hills were deficient."[29]

Some of the Angamis were said to have joined the *Ahom* army.[30] Often when there was a fight between two or more claimants to the throne of Assam, the weaker ones sought refuge in Naga Hills.[31] Even Atan Borgohain, who was the Prime Minister of *Ahom* from 1662-1669 also seems to have taken refuge in Naga Hills.[32]

However, this period of Ahom rule in Assam did not register serious change in Kohima social organization.

---

29. Lakshmi Devi, *op.cit.*, pp. 19-20.
30. Salhouthie Miachieo (70) of Kohima village told instances of Kohima villagers who joined the Ahom army in the past.
31. S.K. Bhuyan, *Atan Borgohain and His Times*, Gauhati, 1965, p. 189.
32. *Ibid.*, pp. 162-163.

Though there was a long drawn process of mutual exchanges, it did not disturb the tribal setting among the Angamis. Prior to the British occupation, the ties of kinship, lineages and clan-based organization did not promote the mobility of the Angamis outside the region. Hence such measures kept tribal social organization uninfluenced and restricted the penetration of outside economy. The Ahom rule which was based on an exploitative structure could not resist the Burmese onslaught and it was in the nineteenth century that extreme poverty developed. Strong symptoms of deterioration began to surface, but before the final liquidation of the empire the Burmese entered Assam and ruled for some years.[33] It was in this period that colonialism made its appearance in Nagaland. Not merely was the Naga areas important from the strategical point of view to the British but from the material point of view as well, because Naga areas was possessed with rich forest resources, oil fields, large tracts of land for tea plantations and agriculture. Apart from these economic considerations, the colonial masters recognized that this was the main entry point for operations in the interior of the North Eastern region and Burma. Strategically, the Naga Hills provided a natural frontier to the British position in India. There was one of reasons that the British ousted the Burmese and concluded the Treaty of Yandabo under which the entire Burmese possessions of North East India were handed over to the British.[34] All these developments exercised tremendous influence on Kohima and for that matter, on the entire Naga Hills.

Although with these developments, Kohima society entered into a transitional phase gradually assimilating the

---

33. Hem Barua, *The Red River and the Blue Hills*, Gauhati, 1954, p. 2.

34. E.A. Gait, *op.cit.*, pp. 332-340

influence exercised by outside economy, with the decline of Ahom rule, a closed nature of economy was imposed and Kohima seems to have closed its doors to developing contacts from Manipur on one hand, and Assam on the other, for a period until British made Kohima headquarters in the later part of the nineteenth century.[35] Though initially the British entry in the Angami country met with strong resistance, the British were gradually able to establish themselves in Nagaland with their main centre at Kohima.[36] It was with the establishment of colonial rule that Kohima assumed prominence from every point of view, until Kohima became the centre not only of political activity but the hub of the socio-cultural and political life of the Nagas.

1. CLAN ORGANISATION OF KOHIMA

a. Kohima

- 1. Lhisemia
  - a. Huoruotsu
    - Sorhie
    - Liezietsu
    - Kesiezie
    - Rulho
      - Yaotsu
      - Chielietsu
  - b. Tsiara
  - c. Khiepfu
- 2. Tsutuonomia
- 3. Dapfutsumia
- 4. Puchatsumia

b. Tsiara

- Mepfuo
- Tseikha
- Vizonuo
- Yhome
- Dzuvichu

---

35. H.K. Barpujari, *Problem of the Hill Tribes: North-East Forntier*, Gauhati, 1981, pp. 50-69.

36. Robert Reid, *op.cit.*, pp. 99-175.

c. Rhiepfu

- Suokhrie
- Linyu
- Khelietsu
  - Kelio
  - Miachieo
  - Kratsutsu
  - Tsiesotsu
  - Khromo

2. TSUTUONOMIA

- Sekhose
- Belho
- Solo
- Whuorie
- Kuotsu
- Geisuo
- Khemieo

3. DAPFUTSUMIA

- Khezhie
  - Keditsu (a sub-clan)
- Kirekha
- Keretru
- Rhiepfumia
  - Yiese
  - Sachu

4. PUCHATSUMIA

- Usuo
- Kerutsa
- Sote
- Pienyu
- Rame
- Keyho

4

KHONOMA

The village of Khonoma has played an unparalled role in the history of Nagaland. Although a small village situated in harsh and rugged terrain, it had long been considered to be the most powerful and feared in the Naga Hills.[1] Dreaded by the *Zemi* villages for its barbaric and ferocious attacks, it meted out cruel harassment to these villages, and caused the *Zemi* to compare it with a hurricane or storm. It is probable that the word 'Angami' was coined by the *Zemi* from their word 'gami' meaning 'invaders',[2] although this point is strongly disputed by the other Angami groups which have their own version of the origin of the name. The tradition of warfare continued to colonial times when Khonoma stubbornly and valiantly resisted the British advent into the Naga Hills.[3] Khonoma played a most significant role in nurturing the growth of the Naga

---

1. James Jhonstone, *Manipur and the Naga Hills*, Delhi, 1971 (reprint), p. 47.
2. This information was given to the scholar by Haigwang Zeliang of Gaili Village.
3. J. Jhonstone, *op.cit.*

struggle for independence and it is also the village of A Z Phizo, the Father of Naga Nationalism.

The name of the village is derived from *Khwuno,* a native plant which grows wild in these hills. The original name, *Khwunomia,* meaning 'Men of Khwuno', has come to be called *Khonoma* in more recent times. It is believed that the original name was given by settlers who preceded the present inhabitants, but moved on because they found the climate 'too cold to grow rice'.[4]

When we look at the source materials regarding the formation of Khonoma, the factors appear similar to those that led to the establishment of other Angami villages.[5]

---

4. This information was given by Theyieviso (87) of Khonoma village.
5. Since childhood, the scholar had participated in many festivals and special occasions where the history of Khonoma was narrated and discussed—a usual customary practice from early times. As a child, the scholar attended the *Thehu* (morung), a traditional institution and dormitory where the young boys are taught the culture and traditions of the tribe by the elders. For over a decade, the author had interviewed hundreds of people in Khonoma with a specific purpose in mind. It is impossible to mention all their names. Listed below are a few names of persons representing various clans who narrated the history of Khonoma to the scholar.
   Bizo (62), *Gaon Bura* of Thevoa clan.
   Dietho-u (63), of Thevom clan.
   Khotonyu (61), of Thevoma clan.
   Yieto (90), of Thevoma clan.
   Visieu (65), of Thevoma clan.
   Visesie (45), of Thevoma clan.
   Theyievizo (87), *Gaon Bura* of Merhuma clan.
   Pusieto (68), *Gaon Bura* of Semoma clan.
   Keriu (60), of Semoma clan.
   Khu-u (69), of Kuthotsu clan.
   Vivor (80), of Kuotsu clan.
   Krulhubi (65), of Semoma clan.
   Petenihu (48), Merhuma clan.
   Thoniu (48), Merhuma clan.
   Sebi (62), Merhuma clan.

Khonoma is situated in the extreme west of Angami country. Although most of the area is mountainous, Khonoma also has considerable stretches of valleys within the hill tracts. The various hills determining the nature and topography of Khonoma are *Ho Phera, Mhoziekha, Nikriba, Sikhri, Virhiecha, Gagidzuthi, Thekhwecathi* and *Kradi.* In the south, Khonoma borders the *Zemi* territory and the romantic *Dzuku* Valley which stretches to Manipur.[6] The northern side faces *Zubza,* and in the east is the village of *Jotsoma* while the village of *Mezoma* lies to the west.

The population of Khonoma is around 6000.[7] The village land stretches to over 20 km in length from east to west. The whole area is rich in forest resources and has innumerable varieties of trees. The forests are of a mixed deciduous and evergreen type, with vast areas of jhum-stands predominated by *Alnus Nepalensis,* locally known as *Rupo.* Among the varieties of forest products, *Rupo,* Alnus Nepalensis, occupies a dominant portion. *Rupo* is popularly known as *alder*. The tree plays a very important role in the economy of Khonoma. It has a unique capacity for regeneration. After felling, when the stump of the tree is so treated by the villagers so as to allow fresh shoots to grow out of the cut stump, five to ten such shoots sprout up

---

6. Unfortunately, there is a serious lack of detailed geographical accounts on Nagaland. Evidence of the village boundaries has been derived from the long fieldwork carried out in the area of study.
7. According to the Khonoma Baptist Church Census 1985, out of the total population of a little over 6000, only 1945 were living in Khonoma in August, 1985. This shows that more than half of the population were living outside the village. Many have jobs in Kohima and others have migrated elsewhere—mostly to Dimapur area, but most of them keep a close link with the village and are registered in the church membership and electoral rolls. This makes it extremely difficult to give the precise population of Khonoma.

from each stump. These then grow to maturity within a period of three years after which they are cut for firewood. This leaves the stump of the tree ready again for the growth of a fresh batch of shoots. Since the cycle of jhum cultivation follows a three-year course, the next harvest of firewood would be again after three years. However, if larger branches are desired, the tree may be cut instead after six years, i.e. during the next jhum cycle. In addition, the alder plays an important ecological role in maintaining the balance of the fertility of the soil. Its leaves serve to form a rich natural layer of topsoil. Almost all the hills have a young sedimentary rock formation and there is a possibility of coal and uranium in some areas.[8] Climatically, the area is pleasant although winter can be cold with mild snowfall on the hilltops. However, the factor which seems to have proved a major attraction for settlers is the terrain of Khonoma which provided large scope for terrace cultivation, and the steep hills, particularly *Mhoziekha*, which provided a natural defence. The terrace cultivation is considered to be a great achievement in Angami civilization. "The unique rice terraces, built through centuries, are famous for their advanced engineering."[9]

Since the beginning of human history, the search for food has been part of the struggle for survival among all

---

8. Unpublished Official Records, Department of Geology and Mining, Government of Nagaland, Kohima.
9. Keviselie Hans Ragnar Mathisen, *Arbervirolas Naga Mussihkka*, Tromso, 1985, p. 8.
   See also C. von Furer-Haimendorf, "Nagas" in *The Illustrated Encyclopedia of Mankind*, Vol II, London, 1978, p. 1424.
   "The Angami... have developed a system of irrigated rice terraces second only to the famous terrace fields of the Ifugo of the Philippines. The Angami terraces are remarkable feats of engineering, carved out of hills slopes over drops of thousands of feet".

peoples. As we discussed in the chapter on Migration and Settlement. *Koza's* descendants went out of Khezhakenoma and formed various villages and tribes in the Naga Hills. One of his descendants was *Vadio*. Tradition narrates that Vadio's sons *Zuonuo* and *Keyhonuo* founded the villages of Southern Angami and formed the Zuonuo-Keyhonuo clans.[10] One of their descendants by the name *Mekhu* lived in Kigwema village.[11] *Mekhu* had two sons—*Merhu* and *Pfukha*. *Pfukha* is said to have lived and died in *Kigwema* but his brother *Merhu* migrated to Khonoma with his youngest son, *Meyase,* following his two other sons, *Khwukha* and *Khate,* who were among the founding fathers of Khonoma.[12] The oral history of the village records that it was during a hunting expedition that *Khwukha* and *Khat* discovered *Khonoma*.[13] It is indicated that the emergence of Khonoma into a village settlement was due to the fact that the Naga indigenous organization depended by and large on hunting for their subsistence, although afforts were also made to supplement it by agriculture. After *Khwukha*'s and

---

10. N.K. Das, "Land Management, Dual inheritance and Redistribution Among the Zuonuo-Keyhonuo Naga", *Agrarian Situation in India*, Vol. I, Calcutta, 1982, p. 85. This evidence is collaborated by oral sources as well.
11. Visa, an old man of 79 years, from Kigwema village, is a traditional storyteller and was kind enough to give this information.
12. Please see the geneological table at the end of this chapter.
13. There are many different versions regarding the history of Khonoma which is a sensitive issue, and each clan stands firmly on its own version. The different interpretations can even lead to clan feuds, the author has come across many heated arguments on this matter in the course of his studies. However, after cross examination of all these versions, the scholar has been in a position to evolve some sort of consensus which was accepted in the light of historical details by almost all the clans of Khonoma and this stands devoid of any traditional bias.

Khate's visit to Khonoma site, the two brothers were convinced that the establishment of a village was not possible without joining hands with some more members. They immediately went to *Jotsoma* and invited one *Ratsa* and his brother *Vokha* to join them.[14]

We find that when *Khwukha* and *Khate* contacted *Ratsa* and *Voka*, the latter could not come immediately because he was wounded in a war. From this evidence we can strongly postulate that these early settlers were active participants in inter-village feuds. Contacting *Ratsa* was not without significance. It seems probable that since these brothers had been involved and perhaps defeated in a feud and since *Vokha* was wounded, they would be open to the idea of establishing a new settlement. Giving shelter to co-tribesmen, on *Khate* and *Khwukha*'s part, would be counted as a point of merit, because in doing so, they would also be gaining the allegiance and loyalty of those persons needed in the formation of a new village. The settlement would require manpower for its protection as well as for its habitation. Thus, once they had chosen Khonoma as a potentially advantageous site for settlement, they lost no time in inviting those people who would be able to fulfill the various roles needed in establishing the new village.[15]

When *Ratsa* decided to accompany *Khate* and *Khwukha* to Khonoma, an agreement was arrived at amongst them: they were to set off on their journey together and each member was to carry a load consisting of exactly the same

---

14. For founding a new village, a long-standing tradition among the Angamis is to invite more people from neighbouring villages.
15. Even in a tribal social formation, when a village settlement on a permanent basis was founded, it required many men and materials not merely for the development of the village, but more so for protecting it from other clans or tribes.

number of belongings so as to ensure that they all started on an equal footing materially in the new village. This points to the basically democratic nature of early indigenous society where equality in all its aspects was greatly valued. However, they stopped on the way and checked each other's luggage, and it was discovered that *Khwukha* had hidden an extra skin of goat's hair in his shield.[16] The presence of this akin of hair led to a prophecy that *Khwukha's* descendants would be blessed and that out of his clan would arise the heroes of the new village.[17]

The founding of this new village was accompanied by many such human episodes and incidents which have been recounted and passed down to the present generation.[18] These incidents formed the basis for prophecies regarding the clans and village life which, strangely enough, have proved creditable enough to be still taken seriously by the villagers to this day. In the face of these prophecies and legends, one cannot discount the view that although the move to Khonoma was motivated by a search for improved material conditions, the early settlers also believed that they were led by the Spirits in their selection of a new home. For instance, as they approached Khonoma, one of the members of the party lost a packet of salt. A search ensued

---

16. Goats were considered sacred animals and the possession of their hair was considered as precious and a sign of good luck. It is possible that *Khwukha* secreted the skin of goat's hair in the superstitious hope that the extra hair he carried would bring him additional blessings.
17. "Tsiesie rei Khwukha dzupuo Khwunoria sier sier tuo derei kemelha lievi" meaning "from Khwukha's clan will emerge heroes, but they will be arrogant."
    Narrated by Pfukolie Khwukha (85) of Khonoma.
18. As Jan Vansina has observed, culture is carried from generation to generation through memory related into words and deeds.
    Jan Vansina, *Oral Trdition as History, op.cit.*, p. xi.

and the culprit was found. It was then foretold that there would be cases of theft in the village but in each case the culprit would not escape undetected.[19] Again, according to Angami tradition, the settlers brought with them sacred chickens with which to consecrate the founding of the village through a ritual called *'phesevu'*. A number of rituals and sacrifices were involved in the consecration of a new village. Sacred chickens were used for these rituals. But when the chickens were let out of their baskets, they began fighting with each other, signifying that there would be enmity and inter-clan feuds within the village. Because of this, *Khate* decided to settle on a hill-top in order to have the advantage should fighting ever break out.[20]

Tradition tells us that the leader of the group first arrived at the spot and unearthed a stone under which he found numerous crabs. This led him to foretell that the people would multiply in this land. He called out to his friends saying,

> "The land worthy of habitation, the land of beauty and goodness, the land free of plague, the land that shall be victorious in war—here is the land we have been seeking. Come, O my people.[21]

Then his companions gathered around him and he recited a prayer to consecrate the foundation of the new village. A simple translation of the prayer goes like this:

---

19. "Tsiesie rei Khwunoria gudi sier rei telie lie tie ha, sidi pupie jushie' meaning "There will be thieves in this land but the culprit would not escape".
20. *Op.cit.*, Folklore of Khonoma.
21. Khonoma Folklore.
    See also *Khonoma Baptist Church Centenary Committee Report*, 12th April 1987. Recorded by Tsiau Terhuja, Sebi Dolie and Thinou Seyie on behalf of the Centenary Committee. Translated by Easterine Iralu. See appendix for original text.

> "The gods have destined that this land shall be ours. We shall dwell here happily and prosper. Here young maidens shall sit and weave and children spin their tops to their hearts content. Our seed shall multiply and fill this land. It shall be a land where rice abounds and the wine vats overflow, where joy and contentment fill every heart and the songs of victory resound over the earth. No plague shall touch it nor famine enter it. Life in this villge shall be the envy of all others. Response: It shall be so."[22]

Moving into the village, each settler selected the site for his house and these traditional sites have remained with their descendants to the present day. In selecting his land, *Ratsa* was given instructions by his brother, *Vokha,* to settle on that land which he had already chosen—an area which had *thekre* (a kind of native plant) and *megu* (a local tree) and which was watered by a perennial spring. However, when *Ratsa* reached Khonoma, he mistook the site and instead settled down on a piece of land that was similar to the one *Vokha* had described although not as good or lush (this is the present *Semomma* land). When *Vokha,* recovering from his war wounds, finally reached Khonoma, he found to his anger that his brother had not settled down in the land that he had selected and instead, the land he wanted was now occupied by other clans.[23] In frustration and anger he cursed the land of his original choice. To this day the descendants of *Vokha* and *Ratsa* believe that this land, *Hiekhakikie,* still bears the curse of *Vokha,* and that this curse would overtake anyone settling on this land. "Tsiesie rei ase ayie mia bu luju ha lhoukenyu" meaning "Cursed be any of my descendants who would live on this land."[24]

22. *Ibid*. Appendix for original text.
23. The reference is obviously to the clan of *Khwukka* and *Khate*.
24. Khonoma Folklore, narrated by Keriu Mor of Semoma clan of Khonoma

There is a host of other stories and episodes connected with the settlement of Khonoma, but these would not be relevant to our discussion at this stage. Whether we can attribute the settlement of Khonoma village to these legends alone this again subjected to doubt because according to Angami clan organization there are two moieties: *Thekrunomia* and *Thevomia* also known as *Thepa\Thevo* or *Kepepfumia* and *Kepezomia*. To understand the various internal mechanisms of the Angami social structure, one should very carefully examine the literature that we derive from various kinds of written or oral information. The Angami legends say that they sprang from two brothers—*Thevo* and *Thekruno*. The growth of population and many other intricacies divided Angamis into various clans but all these clans are identified under these two divisions. One group of clans animated and multiplied from the branch of *Thevo* and the other from *Thekruno*. This dual division of Angami social organization of *Thevomia* and *Thekrunomia*, also *known* as *Kepepfumia* and *Kepezomia* was termed as *kelhu* to avoid confusion. There are complicated intricacies involved in the division of these moieties, especially in the breaking-down of phratries, clans, lineages and kinships, i.e., *thino* and *pfutsa*.

So far as the Angami traditions and religion are concerned, people from one moiety alone could not form a village. The entire history of Angami village formation supports this statement. Participation of the other moiety was a must for the growth of a village because each moiety had a different ritual to perform. For instance, in any religious or social ceremony, it was required that the members of the *Thevomia* had to first partake of the food before the rest of the village could eat. This practice is strictly followed even to this day. So, although *Khwukha, Khate* and *Ratsa* were regarded as the founding fathers of Khonoma, we have no definite evidence to this effect because all these men belonged to *Thekrunomia* moiety. Thus we cannot depend solely on the information extracted from folklore. Probably we can afford to say that it could be that *Khwukha, Khate* and *Ratsa* came first to explore the suitability of Khonoma for settlement, and perhaps shifted to the area, but that Khonoma became a full-fledged village only when the clans of the other moiety joined them.[25]

Looking at the present nature of clan structure in Khonoma, we find that the entire population is divided into three major clans (*thino*): *Merhu, Semo* and *Thevo.*[26] Of these, *Merhu* and *Semo* belong to the *Thekrunomia* moiety, while *Thevo* belongs to the *Thevomia* moiety. As we have demons-trated earlier, *Khwukha, Khate* and *Ratsu* were the first settlers in Khonoma. But the presence of the *Thevomia* moiety in the present structure proves that the formation of the village was completed only when the members of that moiety came to the village. Although there are slight variations in these narrations, the history of the first settlers form the fabric of a common knowledge as the villagers have grown up hearing these tales at their firesides and festive occasions.

---

25. The concept of village formation has been discussed by various scholars on the basis of their empirical situations. Since we are not discussing village formation on conceptual lines, the discussion shall, therefore remain limited in this area. Vansina has done a valuable work on this aspect. Jan Vansina, *Kingdoms of the Savanna, op.cit.*
26. The exact number of clans which have branched out from the Angami tribe cannot be established as yet, because the analysis of this aspect involves some complexities. In the recent history, the growth of population and other opportunities of business and employment through the process of modernization has shaken the very foundations of clan-based relations, and many more sub-clans have been formed. For instance, *Putsure, Vizol, Kevichusa* and so on are very recently formed sub-clans. So to give the number of clans will not be appropriate in this respect.

A study of the formation of each of these clans would be necessary at this point.

MERHU — As already indicated, the *Merhu* clan consisted of the descendants of *Merhu* through his sons, *Khate, Khwukha* and *Meyase.* In addition there was another section of the *Merhu* clan who owed their origin to *Nriu.*[27] *Nriu* was the adopted son of *Pfukha,* brother of *Merhu.* Although *Nriu* himself did not settle in Khonoma, his son and grandsons were brought to the village by *Khate.* The section of the *Merhu* clan which has originated from *Nriu* has played a very important role in the history of Khonoma. Therefore it is necessary to probe into the circumstances that led to *Nriu*'s adoption and the subsequent migration of his descendants to Khonoma.

Nriu was an orphan turned legend. He was of the *Zemi* tribe of *Tsiekwuma* village. He was brought up by his brother but his sister-in-law seriously ill-treated him, compelling him to leave his brother's house to fend for hemself. *Nriu* was a hard working man, proficient in the art of agriculture. As the fruit of his labour he harvested a hundred baskets of millet single-handed which was a great achievement in his village given the nature of the means of production at that time. To mark his achievement, he announced that he would perform a Feast of Merit. But his sister-in-law, in her jealousy at his growing importance, burnt down his barns and *Nriu* was forced to leave the village. This disappointment made him to chose the path of an ascetic which was completely divorced from material culture, and he dwelt in the romantic *Dzuku Valley* living on wild fruits and vegetable from the forest. *Dzuku* which

27. The oral literature is replete with various references to *Nriu.* He seems to have played a significant role in the evolution of some of the traditions which are still held by the Angamis with great reverence and regard to *Nriu.*

means 'cool water' is a valley in the frontier of Manipur and Nagaland. Abundant in wild animals, flowers and fruits, it has a wild and haunting beauty. Many legends and myths are connected with this place.

One day, *Pfukha* and his friend, *Seca* found *Nriu* in the valley and brought him home to their village *Kigwema*. Both the friends wanted to adopt *Nriu* and so entered into an agreement as to who would adopt him. They decided that the one whom *Nriu* first addressed as *'Apfu'* or 'father' would have the right to adopt him. After this, Seca took *Nriu* home, but the young man never spoke a word. *Pfukha* then had his turn of keeping *Nriu*. Here too, *Nriu* was silent for many days until one day, *Pfukha* came home with many birds which he had trapped. His other children thronged around him calling out to him. He rewarded them with a bird each. *Nriu* watching the scene, was moved to also utter the word *'Apfu'* or 'father' whereupon he received his share of the hunt. *Pfukha,* according to the agreement then adopted him.[28]

Nriu lived in the house of *Pfukha* until one day, *Pfukha*'s daughter, *Thuuse,* received an offer of marriage from *Merhiese* of *Secuma* village. The marriage was arranged and *Nriu* was sent to accompany his foster-sister to her new home. For this reason, to this day, the descendants of Nriu are known as 'the descendants of the one who washed the hands of *Thuuse*'[29] He found favour with the villagers of *Secuma* and grew in popularity. When the time for his return came, the villagers refused to let him go back. Oral

---

28. Khonoma villagers, *op.cit*.
29. The descendants of *Nriu* are known in Angami as "Thuuse bitinuo yiemia" which literally means "descendants of the person who washed the hands of *Thuus*". This title had adhered because according to folklore, *Pfukha* sent his adopted son, *Nriu*, along with his daughter as a servant.

sources say that *Pfukha* sent his men three times to *Secuma* to bring back *Nriu*. But the *Secuma* villagers refused to let him go back, and instead sent gifts including conch shells to *Pfukha* through his men. Pfukha was furious with his men for accepting the gifts, but after a time he realized the futility of trying to get *Nriu* to come back.

Ultimately he married and settled there and had two sons—*Thorenyu* and *Soru*. *Thorenyu* had two sons—*Gwizanu* and *Lievuse*. *Gwizanu* became the priest of *Secuma* and died there. But his sons and brother, *Lievuse*, were brought to Khonoma by *Khate*. It is of great significance that Nriu's son *Gwizanu* became the chief priest (*Zievo*) of Secuma. It must have been a great achievement on the part of *Gwizanu* to have acquired such an important position and status as one who would be considered as a newcomer.

Thus it came to pass that the descendants of *Nriu* came to Khonoma and increased in number and their prosperity grew. Their contribution proved a major factor in the building of Khonoma into a powerful village. It is appropriate to mention that the famous Naga Nationalist leader, Mr. A.Z. Phizo, is a direct descendant of Nriu, who has played a key role similar to his ancestor in shaping the history of Nagaland.

SEMO — The second clan that has significantly contributed to the growth of Khonoma was the *Semo* clan. This clan consists of two phratries—*Chalieutsu* and *Kuthotsu*.[30] *Chalieu* was the father of *Ratsa* and *Vokha*, the first settlers. Although he himself did not come Khonoma, the clan, descended through *Ratsa* and *Vokha*, retains his name. The other subclans of *Chalieutsu* are *Mor*, *Rulho* and *Seyie*.[31]

---

30. The suffix 'tsu' such as in Chalieu*tsu* and Kutho*tsu* means grandson or in general usage, descendants. Thus, the word '*Chalieutsu*' would mean 'descendants of Chalieu'.
31. Ulalhou Vupru (50) of Semoma clan, Khonoma, gave this information.

The *Kuthotsu* phratry was named after *Kutho* who came to Khonoma from Secuma village.[32] The sub-clans of this phratry are—*Vupru, Secu, Zhunyu* and *Rurhie.* An interesting point to note is that *Kutho* for whom the clan is named is actually not the originator of the clan. The clan was originally founded by two other men—*Pelevi* from *Secuma* village and *Hiesenu* from Jotsoma village. When *Kutho* came to Khonoma he allied himself with them. But in course of time he and his descendants became more influential, overshadowing the members of *Pelevi* and *Hiesenu.* The result was that the clan acquired his name. This illustrates that the clan or sub-clans does not always bear the name of its originator, but sometimes chooses to call itself after a more popular or illustrious person who may join the clan at a later stage.

THEVO — The type of clan emergence mentioned above also occurred within the *Thevo* clan. The sub-clans of this clan today are—*Chatsu, Phetsu* and *Kotsu*. However, the first settlers belonging to the Thevo clan who came to Khonoma were *Kehiekha* and *Keviso,* who came from Merema village.[33] As mentioned earlier, *Thevo* clan forms part of *Thevomia* moiety, the presence of which was imperative to fulfill the ritual requirements involved in the establishment of a village. It was *Kehiekha* and *Keviso,* as members of this moiety, who were invited to settle in Khonoma for the purpose of fulfilling these obligations. But today their descendants are united under one clan called *Chatsu,* descended from *Necha* of *Merema*. The *Phetsu* clan consists of three divisions of kinships—*Kruse, Pieru* and

32. *Secuma* is an ancient Angami village near *Mezoma,* in the western Angami sector. Once it was a powerful village but is now reduced to a small village of about 40 houses.

33. Diethou (65) of Chatsu clan, Khonoma, gave this information.

Yalie. This clan was founded by a man called *Pfuphe* who came to *Khonoma* from *Kiruphe* village.[34]

Ko, the founder of *Kotsu* clan, came from a place called *Kojuzhu*, a place near Kohima village.[35] When *Ko* heard that a new village, Khonoma, was being founded he was eager to settle there too. However, he was delayed as he had to perform a Feast of merit *(Jashu)*. Also, tradition required that any man who wished to leave a village to settle in a new village after giving Feast of Merit had to perform certain harvest rituals. He thus had to grow and harvest a crop before he could leave for Khonoma, after performing the necessary rites.[36]

Once these major clans—*Merhu, Semo* and *Thevo*—settled in Khonoma, other sub-clans, phratries,lineages and kinships continued to emerge and multiply to form the present intricate network of clan structure and relationship which affects the affairs of the village to this day.[37]

The emergence of chieftainship, *Peyumia,* played a

---

34. Visesie (46) Phetsu clan, Khonoma, gave this information.
35. Vivor (81) the oldest member of Kotsu clan, traditional storyteller, narrated this. The ancient Kojuzhu village is now the site of the present 'Little Flower School', Kohima.
36. In a society where agriculture is predominant, sowing and harvesting often form the basis of religious ceremonies.
37. These developments indicate the gradual promotion of material resources of the tribe which ran parallel to the growth of population. In fact, at this stage the lack of improvement in technology and non-incorporation of external influences seems to have been a major reason for not transforming the growing clans into a state structure of any degree. In other parts of India, it was at this stage that the application of the varna system worked as a dissolving influence for transforming the tribal structure. It was the varna system which expanded the social division of labour and laid the foundation of a stratified social order. B.N.S. Yadav, *Society and Culture in Northern India*, Allahabad, 1972, pp. 1-76.

unique role in consolidating Angami tribal social organization.

> "The Nagas are republicans and their peumahs, or chiefs are elected, and though they often have great influence, they are in theory only, Primus inter pares, and are liable at any time to be displaced. Practically, they often remain in office for years and are greatly respected".[38]

The term *peyumia* has been loosely translated as 'chieftain'. But one may differ on this point. There are some characteristics that differentiate them from, say, the Mizos or the Khasis.[39] In these tribes the chiefs, by and large, depended on the mode of selection or election, *i.e.* chiefs are generally hereditary or elected by the people. But what may be pointed out here is that the Angami *peyumia* were neither from a hereditary lineage nor were they the result of a search for the election of a leader.[40] The *Peyumia*, rather, were those who emerged naturally as respected and recognized leaders. The basis for such an emergence could be personal charisma, integrity of character, power of oratory, diplomacy, physical prowess and skill in war, wisdom and wealth. A combination of some of these traits would make a man stand out in society as a *peyumia*. Once a man was accepted as a *peyumia*, he had considerable power and influence, the strength of which did not follow any regulated jurisdiction but rather rested on the strength of his own individual achievements and personality. Thus, it was quite possible for a number of *Peyumia* to co-exist at one time in a single village and to work in co-operation with each other, if they all proved themselves possessed of the criteria required. The *peyumia*, one or many, had a

38. J. Johnstone, *op.cit.*, p. 28.
39. P.R.T. Gurdon, *The Khasis*, Calcutta, 1914.
40. From the village informants of Khonoma, *op.cit.*

strong voice on all matters regarding governing of the village and related affairs. But although the *peyumia* would wield great powers, the very mode of emergence dictated that the basic indigenous democratic structure was not disturbed or displaced. A well-known *peyumia* of Khonoma village was *Pelhu* under whose leadership Khonoma invaded and plundered *Gariphe* village in the middle of the 19th century. In 1880, after the famous Battle of Khonoma, when a Peace Treaty was made with the British, the leader of the Khonoma delegation was again Pelhu, who was now an old man. After Khonoma was annexed, the British made Pelhu the first *Gaonbura* (village headman) of Khonoma, thus starting the office of the *Gaonbura* which became a very powerful and influential position for nearly a century until the creation of Nagaland State in 1963.It was the creation of the office of the *Gaonbura* that more or less displaced the traditional system of *peyumia*.[41]

The steady and sure supply of food and the availability of large tracts of land led to the growth of population in course of time. This increased the labour force which brought more lands under terrace cultivation and also provided security from the other tribes as well. It was here that the first preliminaries of division of labour sprang

---

41. Here it comes closer to *Gamo* society of South Africa where in an assembly each citizen had the right to express himself freely. The decisions were adopted unanimously by taking a vote and counting of voices. But what makes the Angami *Peyumia* distinct from the institution *Gamo* society is that the latter, the institution had the right to punish those who refused to obey their authority, which did not exist among Angamis. Therefore the Angami society seems to have been possessed of actual democratic norms.
Mark Abeles, "In Search of Monarch: Introduction of State among Gamo of Ethiopia" in *Modes of Production in South Africa*, edited by D. Grummey and C.C. Stewart, 12 Vols, 1981, pp. 51-53.

up.[42] Besides, the location of Angami country, particularly its nearness to the plains of Assam and Manipur, brought the Angamis into contact with other peoples and cultures. Thus came in the new skills both of craftsmanship and agriculture and strengthened the social differentiation. However, the multiplication of population did not mean the diffusion of tribal social organization altogether. The increasing population led to the formation of new clans and sub-clans mushrooming new *peyumias*. For example, when *Meyase* came to Khonoma, he became the originator of the Meyase clan. In course of time as the population increased, the descendants of his sons formed six sub-clans or kinships of *Zetsuvi, Kenieu, Khwukha, Pfulise, Sanyu* and *Iralu*. It appears that the establishment of Khonoma itself nursed the ascending wave of Angami influence. From Khonoma they began to extend their area of influence by bringing some neighbouring tribes under control by force and persuasion. The basic fundamentals of statecraft at this stage were not developed at all. But paying tribute was considered an important symbol of subordination and recognition of one's authority.[43]

---

42. We do not deny the fact that prior to this growth of population no division existed in the Angami society. There was a rudimentary differentiation, which evolved on the basis of ritual tendency, priesthood, wealth, warriorship and some other aspect similar to the one illustrated by Laibman in his analysis.
David Laibman, *op.cit.*, pp. 257-273.
43. An analysis of state formation made by Romila Thapar is useful while studying such situations. But unfortunately the Angamis had a non-state society which will manifest itself in our analysis. There must have existed some arrangement for collection of tribute from other tribes. It appears that, usually, that no organized or preliminary machinery for tribute existed. It was the individual affair of various Angami chiefs bordering non-Angami tribes. As a result these relations could not be formalized as has been discussed by Romila Thapar. R. Thapar, *op.cit.*, pp. 11-13.

This extension of authority could not have been so easily effected. It must have involved a lot of conflicts and fighting among various tribes and clans. The people of Khonoma were in receipt of tribute from some villages of other tribes particularly the *Zeliangs*.[44] It was this important factor which later convinced the British to come to terms with Khonoma Angami, which, of course, at first proved to be a difficult task. The practice of tribute collection, extortion of services and contribution from various tribes did not merely provide security to these tribes but also helped the growth of economic organization and division of labour among the Angamis. The mechanism of collecting dues from various non-Angami villages was a surplus appropriated by the *peyumia* systematically. Since the level of consumption was not high in the Naga Hills given the nature of society, the early Angamis exchanged commodities like cotton, ginger, salt, woven cloths etc. for iron which was used for fighting, hunting and agricultural equipments.[45]

The terrace cultivation in Khonoma certainly required a more improved technology than what was required in jhum cultivation. The regular labour services of men and in some cases slaves were utilized. The phenomenon of slavery as such did not exist in Khonoma or for that matter in the entire Angami society. When we refer to slaves there are some isolated cases when they forcibly captured men and women of other villages or tribes and employed them in such tasks to earn their livelihood but there did not exist any slave market

---

44. J.H. Hutton, *op.cit.*, p. 252. "These tribes are situated to the south of the Angamis and have been very much influenced by them. The Zemi having been long virtually subject to the Angami village of Khonoma."
45. Lakshmi Devi, *op.cit.*, pp. 19-20.

nor an economy based on slavery as was in the case of Roman society.[46] Small canals from streams were cut across the hills for irrigation of fields and other purposes.[47] Other activities included weeding, ploughing, harvesting, cutting of wood and so on. All these developments gradually improved the living standard of the Khonoma people in particular and the Angami in general. These measures led to further growth of population because more people would have meant more labour and productivity at that time. The regulation of irrigation, the supervision of the process of production and appropriation, the conduct of war affairs and the other general activities gave birth to a kind of administrative organism.[48] Within the clans obviously the numbers increased and formed sub-clans which went on multiplying. They owed their allegiance to clan elders by assisting in various works assigned to them thereby giving impetus to clan multiplication.

Gradually, it seems that the power and authority of Khonoma increased to such an extent that even neighbouring rajas and chiefs were apprehensive of their attacks.[49]

---

46. M Gibbs, *Feudal order*, London 1949. Barry Hindess and Paul Q. Hirst. *Pre-Capitalist Mode of Production*, London, 1975, pp. 109-147.
47. The canals were cut with labour from the rivers of *Dzuyieru, Krukhruru, Dzuza, Khwunodzukhuru, Khuru* which are fed by natural sources. *These* facts were verified by field work conducted by the scholar.
48. In such an administrative organism the authority was regulated and supervised by the *Peyumia* and this did not develop to a state level and does not therefore qualify under the elements of early state as discussed by Henri J.M. Claessen and P. Skalnick in *The Early Stage, op.cit*. See also H.J.M. Claessen, "The Internal Dynamics of early State" in *Current Anthropology*, Vol. 25, No. 4, Aug.Oct. 1984, pp. 365-370.
49. With the increase in their numbers the Angamis went on subjecting their neighbouring villages and thereby raised voluntary contingents for furtherance of their authority.

Possibly it was because of this expanding power that the Dimasa Raja offered one of his daughters to an Angami clan leader in an attempt to forestall the liquidation of his authority.[50] Matrimonial ties have been an assurance of security and friendship between various principalities from ancient times.

Now, Khonoma had built up a kind of state apparatus without dissolving the indigenous organization. It was at this stage of development that there emerged some heroic personalities who excelled in various facets of human activity—some were skilled in warfare, others in the art of agriculture. Some attained distinction as soldiers, still more as craftsmen and men of art. There is an abundance of folklore on the subject with some exaggeration of course. But a careful examination does provide us with valuable historical examples.

For instance, the legend of *Yalie* is notable. There are a number of legends which illustrate his courage, skills and knowledge.[51] Two of the most well known of these narrate his exploits in killing a tiger single-handed and plundering *Lakiema*, a Zemi village. In the second instance, he forced the people of Lakiema village to pay tribute to Khonoma.

Likewise, *Meruno* went to the Ahom king in disguise and confirmed many details of trade and commercial prospects. Folklore tells us that *Meruno* traded in gold, a commodity hitherto unknown to the Angamis. He emerged

---

50. Khonoma village informants, *op.cit.*
51. The legend of Yalie is common knowledge in Khonoma. There is still a huge monolith which was erected under the supervision of Yalie. It is called "Yalie tsie" which means "Yalies's stone."

as one of the first Angami merchants and introduced good trade relations with the Manipuris.[52]

There are also many instances where Khonoma had plundered and invaded a number of villages. One such instance was the war with *Gariphe* village sometime in the middle of the nineteenth century. Khonoma invaded *Gariphe* village and completely razed it to the ground. The heroes of this war, *Pelhu* and *Pukahie*, captured *Saruu*, the most beautiful girl of the village and brought her to Khonoma. A song that *Saruu* composed while living in Khonoma as a captive shows the strengh of Khonoma during that period. A loose translation of the song is as follows:

"Terhuso's sister Saruu
Kidnapped from Garipheju
was taken to Khwunoria,
captive of Pelhu and Pukahie
might warriors both and renowned.

Standing upon that alien land, I thought
Were we both bulls of equal stature
I would have unwaveringly fought you.
You are a full-grown bull
I am but a fledgling calf.
Behind you lie your allies-
The dwellers of Japfu's vales
As mighty as, as terrible as
Spirit-fires burning upon the mountains
Leaving nary a spot unsigned,
You waged war upon me
And I, Defenceless, outnumbered,

---

52. Khonoma folklore. *Meruno* is a fictitious name but his role as a historical character cannot be denied like that William Tell of Switzerland.

Could not withstand your onslaught
But choose instead to yield to your might.[53]

The emergence of these folk heroes not only transformed Khonoma into a very powerful village, but also earned for her higher social standing, elevating the position of her inhabitants. It was through the efforts of these heroes that the Angamis made their presence to the neighbouring territories felt in a forceful and impressive manner.

In this manner, Khonoma grew to enjoy a certain supremacy by its power and strength over other tribal villages. Hutton wrote:

> "It is not without reason that Khonoma, in particular, has been chosen as a typical Angami village. Before the coming of the 'Sarkar' no Angamis enjoyed such widespread tribute as Khonoma. In spite of serious clan dissensions within the village, they were known and feared from Henima to Themokedima, and Razama to the Mikir Hills in Golaghat. Kohima, it is true, were too numerous for Khonoma to attack with any hope of success, and perhaps had the greater influence over the East Angami country and did all the trade on that side. It is only of recent years that Khonoma has taken of trading far afield in that direction. But this hegemony, if it may be called such, of Khonoma, merely meant that Khonoma was stronger than most other villages and consequently bullied and levied a sort of 'Denegelt' wherever it could."[54]

The Khonoma group has also been described as "that group which is generally regarded as being Angami par excellence.[55]

53. Khonoma folk song, translated by Easterine Iralu, see appendix for original text.
54. J.H. Hutton, *op.cit.*, p. 11.
55. *Ibid.*

Geneology of the scholar *Visier, Sanyu*

Tribe: *Angami.* Village: *Khonoma.* Moiety: *Thekrunomia* (Kepefumia) Phratry: *Merhu.* Clan: *Meyase.* Kinship: *Sanyu.*

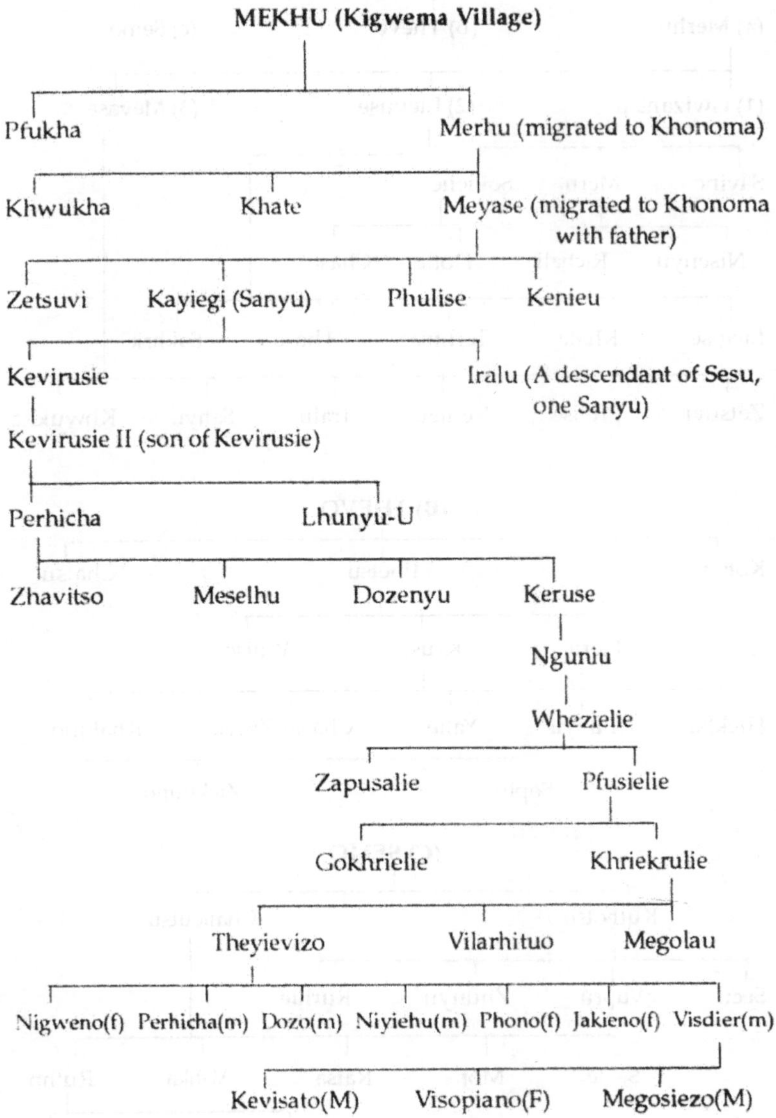

Khonoma Clan Organization

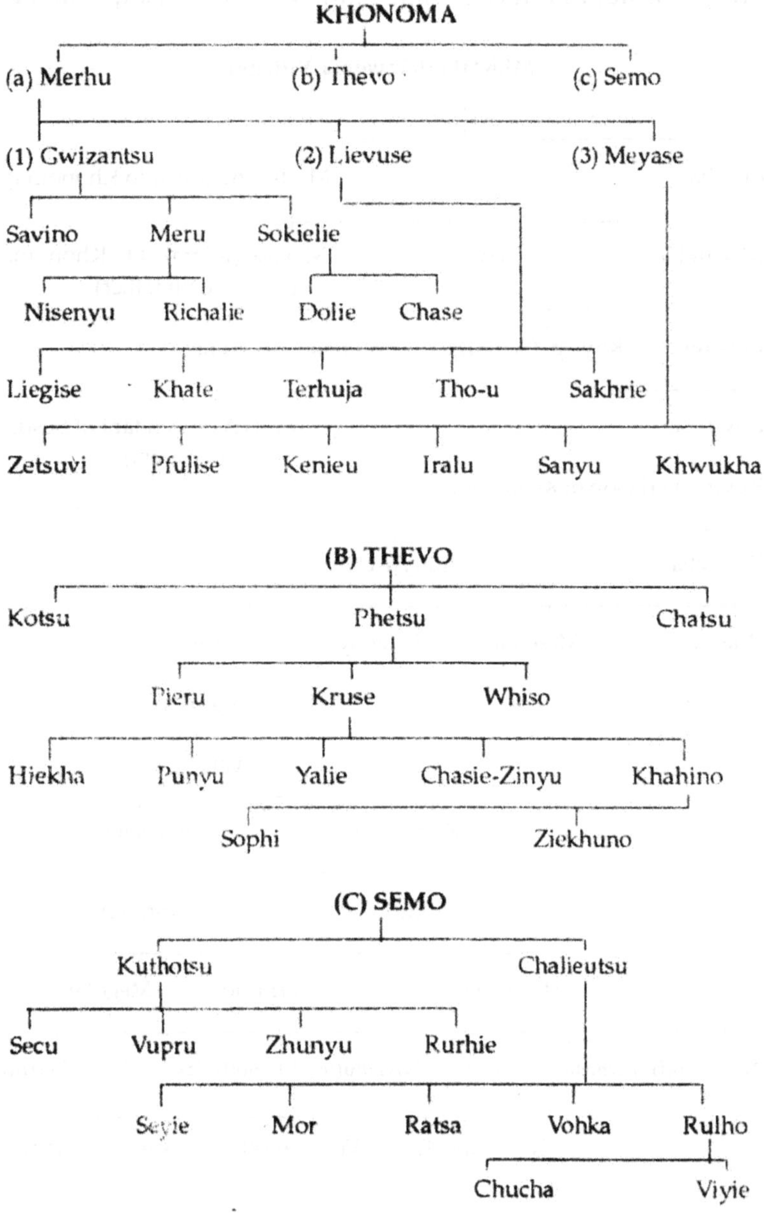

5

BRITISH COLONIZATION

With the commencement of the nineteenth century. British colonialism had touched the highest particularly it terms of territorial expansion and exploitation of resources. The conquest of Bengal after the Battle of Plassey (1757) had given them a great advantage in conquering the rest of India as the rich revenue could be utilized by them.[1] In fact, they did it so schematically that rulers of various parts of India were gradually dislodged to add to the strength of British dominion in India.[2] In the North Western region of India, British colonialism made great progress by liquidating the Sikh rule in Punjab and Kashmir in 1846, trying to establish their residency in Gilgit bordering China.[3] As a

1. R. Mukherjee, *The Rise and Fall of East India Company*, Bombay, 1973, p. 257-268.
2. R.C. Majumdar, *British Paramountancy in Indian Renaissance*, Vol. IX, Part I, Bombay, 1970.
3. The British occupation of Kashmir was desired more from the security point of view. To stop the Russian and Chinese advance the British felt the necessity of containing the Sikh Kingdom.
   F. Drew, *The Northern Barrier of India*, London, 1877. Herbert B. Edwards and M. Herman, *Life of Sir Henry Lawrence, London*, 1873, p. 261. See also R.L. Hangloo, *Agrarian System of Kashmir*, Delhi, 1995, pp. 1-10.

matter of fact, China and Burma figure prominently in British-Indian politics since the beginning of the nineteenth century when they made all-out efforts to promote their mercantile interests.[4] It was this Anglo-Burmese commercial question that lifted the position of North East India very high in British maneuvers.[5]

The North Eastern region was divided into a number of monarchies, kingdoms and village states. Assam, Cachar, Jaintia, Tripura and Manipur were monarchical states.[6] In Khasi Hills there were a number of petty states under *syiemship*.[7] The Naga Hills and Arunachal Pradesh were either under tribal chiefs or managed by the tribal councils and were left untouched by Indians.[8] The British colonists had the advantage in many in annexing the North Eastern region to their empire. The monarchies were on the decline. To make matter worse, in Manipur and Assam there were rival claimants to the throne. The contesting parties sought either British of Burmese intervention.[9] Burma was then a

---

4. M.I. Sladkovsky, *The Long Road: Sino-Russian Economic Contacts from Ancient Times to 1917*, Moscow, 1981, pp. 158-162.
5. H.K. Barpujari, *op.cit.*
   Charles Allen, *A Mountain in Tibet*, London, 1983, pp. 98-119.
6. John Butler, *Travels and Adventures in the Province of Assam*, Delhi, 1985.
   H.K. Barpujari, *Political History of Assam*, Vol. One, Gauhati, 1977, pp. 1-6.
7. Hamlet Bareh, *History and Culture of Khasi People*, Shillong, 1964, pp. 51-134.
   H. Lyngdoh, *Ki Syiem Khasi Synteng bad ka Niam Khasi*, Shillong, 1937.
   P.R.T. Gurdon, *The Khasis*, Calcutta, 1914.
8. H.K. Barpujari, *op.cit.*
9. This was the usual phenomenon with the decline of Ahom power. When the Manipuris drove out the ruler of Cachar, he went to seek British protection and ultimately all such moves by various chiefs and rajahs gave the British the upper hand in subjecting these areas. H.K. Barpujari, *Political History of Assam*, *op.cit.*, p. 5.

powerful state with political ambitions in North East India. The Burmese occupied Assam, Manipur and Cachar.[10] Their army marched towards Jaintia and assumed a stiff attitude towards the British territory of Bengal.[11] In spite of their policy of non-intervention, the British declared war against Burma in March 1824.[12] The Burmese were badly defeated and the British emerged as the most dominant power by the Treaty of Yandabo (1826). Under the terms of this Treaty signed between the king of Ava on the Burmese side and the British, "His Majesty, the king of Ava surrendered among others his claim over Assam and the neighbouring states of Cachar, Jaintia and Manipur to the British."[13]

The occupation of the indigenous territories bordering Assam was now important to the British from various points of view. As J.B. Bhattacharjee puts it,

> "Ever since their ascendancy in Assam valley, the British aimed at using the tribes of eastern fringes as a screen between the newly acquired territories and the kingdom of Burma."[14]

Apart from this strategic position, it was important for commercial reasons as well:

> "The discovery of tea (1823), coal and petroleum (1825), had already impressed upon the company the prospects of promotion of its commercial interests."[15]

10. *Ibid.*, pp. 4-5. See also Asoso Yonou, *op.cit.*, 62-85.
11. H.K. Barpujari, *op.cit.*, pp. 4-5.
12. E.A. Gait, *op.cit.*, pp. 232-240.
13. H.K. Barpujari, *op.cit.*, p. 7.
14. J.B. Bhattacharjee, "The Eastern Himalayan Trade of Assam in the Colonial period", Proceedings of *North East India History Association*, First Session, Shillong, 1980, p. 178.
15. *Ibid.*, p. 179.

Moreover, Assam was exposed to the Naga raids and the British ultimately decided in favour of the forward Policy.[16]

The first British contact with the Nagas was established in 1832 when Francis Jenkins and R.B. Pamberton travelled through the Angami territory in search of a route between Manipur and Assam.[17] To quote Moffat Mills,

> "The first time the Angami Naga country was ever visited by Europeans was January 18, 1832, when Captains Jenkins and Pamberton with a party of 700 soldiers and 800 coolies or porters of carry the baggage and provisions marched from Manipur in progress to Assam. The route pursued was via Sengmae, Myungkhang, Mooran Khoohoo, Moheelong, Dhaseree river, Mohang Dejoa and Ramsah which latter place they reached about the 23rd of January 1832."[18]

Thus the territories inhabited by the Nagas, which first came into contact with the British were those of the Angami

---

16. A Mackenzie, *op.cit.*, 129.
In 1876 Col. R.H. Keatinge, the Chief Commissioner of Assam, with the prior permission of the secretary of State adopted the Forward Policy for preventing future raids and exacting reparation for the past outrages.
Ibid., p. 130.
17. The contact of the British with the Nagas should not be taken to imply that the British established themselves in Naga Hills in 1832, but it was the earliest referenece made in our sources about the British entrance into the Naga Hills in search of a road link between Manipur and Assam. However, their political motivation cannot be ruled out.
18. A.J. Moffat Mills, *Report on the Province of Assam*, 1854, pp. CXLV-CXII.
Political Proceedings, 5th March, 1832, Nos. 67-71, India office Library, London.
See also V. Elwin, *Nagas in the Nineteenth Century*, Bombay, 1969,

tribe. The Angamis, fearing British invasion, put up a tough resistance in the beginning and fought with whatever primitive weapons they had. But the well-organized British forces with the latest and superior fighting weapons finally succeeded in penetrating through the Naga country.[19]

Thereafter, a series of expeditions followed. In 1833, Lieut. Gordon conducted the second expedition.[20] The series of expeditions carried out by the British demonstrate clearly that they could not register much success although they were well equipped in terms of soldiers and armoury. But their frequent attempts laid the foundation for the process of detribalization in the traditional Naga political and social organization.[21] Some years after the expedition of 1833, the Assam Tea Company, which at the time was the most prominent one, established its foothold in areas of Upper Assam Bordering the Naga Hills.[22]

The ex-rajah of Upper Assam, Purander Singha (1836), seems to have felt insecure at this increasing British penetration. He therefore granted the territories of Gabharu Hills in Upper Assam bordering Naga territory to the British.[23] This act proved to be of great significance to the British, because it was from this permanent establishment that they could easily penetrate and make

19. *Ibid*. The Nagas used bows and arrows and spears. They also rolled boulders on the advancing British troops.

20. *Ibid*.

21. It was with the British entrance that the new administration tried to erode the political strength of the traditional tribal institutions by running a kind of parallel system, though extremely limited in the initial phase.

22. The Assam Tea Company was founded by London merchants on 12th Feburary, 1839.
R.C. Majumdar, *op.cit.*, p. 1099.

23. H.K. Barpujari, *op.cit.*, p. 1.

further attempts to subdue the Naga tribes. Here we can rightly say that Rajah Purander Singha opened a constant dispute between the British and the Nagas by his grant of this piece of land.[24] From 1836 to 1879, there followed a number of expeditions under the supervision of various civil officers and military lieutenants.[25] After repeated efforts of Mr. Grange in 1839 and 1840, Lieut. Biggs tried his best to settle the political future of the Nagas. But his efforts succeeded only in settling the border with Manipur in 1842.[26] This was one of the important measures adopted by the British in order to limit the aggressive activities of the Naga raiders in Cachar:

> "the territory was subjected to frequent raids of the Angami Nagas which made even the neighbouring British district wholly insecure."[27]

Realizing the development techniques pursued by the British, some of the prominent Angami clan elders entered into an agreement with the British and agreed to pay annual tribute to them.[28] However, a permanent solution to the problem of British interference could not be worked out.

---

24. It should be noted that Gabharu Hills were not inhabited by the Angamis but by some other Naga tribes who shared the border with Upper Assam, *Ibid.*
25. A Mackenzie, *op.cit.*, pp. 101-148.
26. *Ibid.*, p. 107.
27. H.K. Barpujari, *op.cit.*, p. 30.
    It was probably these raids which forced the Ahoms to grant some amount of arable land to the Nagas earlier. P Gogoi, *op.cit.*, p. 550.
28. No written agreement was signed. Since there were not many resources available in Naga Hills, the British satisfied themselves with the subjugation of some Angami villages which could be ensured merely by payment of tribute. Besides, the British were interested in political subjugation for strategic purposes as already illustrated in the beginning of this chapter. A Mackenzie, *op.cit.*, p. 108.

The chiefs (Peyumia) of Khonoma demonstrated an extremely indifferent attitude towards their neighbour village and clan chiefs of Mezoma in the presence of the British officers.[29] These instances of disunity among the village leaders of Khonoma and Mezoma were taken to be a favourable condition for the advancement of the British interests. But when the British sent their officers only a year later under the supervision of Elds in 1874, with the expectation of collecting tribute, the Angamis not only completely refused but even went to the extent of killing most of the sepoys posted there.[30] This incident was a cause of serious concern for the British. In 1845, John Butler took over the task of conciliating the tribes. He was provided with a reasonably strong force to help him in his venture. But Butler succeeded in carrying out British policy only to a limited extent.[31] Assessing the situation with great care, he adopted a friendly attitude towards the chiefs (Peyumia) which helped him in procuring some items of ivory, cloths and spears as tribute from some of the village. To the Angamis, he was popularly known as 'Zieni Shaha', and was respected and welcomed as an ambassador

---

29. From these indifferences it is evident that the Khonoma elders had not consulted the people of Mezoma and other Angamis before committing themselves to the British. It is possibly this attitude which offended the Mezoma clan chiefs. *Ibid.*
30. *Ibid.* It can be argued that when they made a commitment to the British they did not realize the economic consequences. In a society where resources were limited due to both environmental and technological handicaps, and a new tax (tribute) hitherto unknown was levied, it was but natural to result in a strong protest which could take any form.
31. John Butler, *op.cit.*
See also *Political Proceedings*, 23rd May, 1946, Nos. 30-31, India Office Library, London.

representing the 'White Man's kingdom'.[32] These tribal leaders stated clearly their incapability in collecting the tribute from the tribesmen. Before Butler reappeared in 1846-47, the chiefs continued to indulge in intra-tribal warfare, plunder and other activities. This was enough to give the British as excuse for the establishment of a permanent outpost in the Naga Hills. Butler wrote :

> "I was much amused today at the modest request of the Mozo-mah chief to grant him a guard of twenty sipahees to be stationed in his village when he should be able to fight all his enemies, and he would first commence by taking revenge on Kono-mah."[33]

This was followed by the construction of a road from Mohing Dejoa to Chumukedima and the erecting of godowns for grains and the market place at Dimapur. Bhogchand, a loyal British agent tried to settle the inter-tribal rivalries by advancing the British posts in Mezoma.[34] This underestimation of the strength of the Angamis led to his death at the hands of Angami warriors in Mezoma.[35]

---

32. It is necessary to point out that a lot of misunderstanding has crept into history due to the biased accounts of the British civil servants. Butler for his kind attitude was presented these items as a mark of friendship by a few chiefs but he misinterpreted these gifts as a political submission of the Angamis.
33. John Butler, *op.cit.*, p. 44.
34. A Mackenzie, *op.cit.*, p. 109.
    The in-charge of supervision in Dimapur Market was Bhogchand, a British revenue official. The sources refer to Bhogchand as a *sezawal* but the real term is *sazawul*. One comes across this term in Mughal revenue records. See Abul Fazl, *Akbarnama*, (Persian), 1601, English translation by Agha Ahmed Ali and Abdul Rahmin, Calcutta, 1864. At another Place Mackenzie refers to Bhogchand as a British constable. This shows that Bhogchand was possessed with civil and criminal authority. A Mackenzie, *op.cit.*
35. *Ibid.*, p. 110.

All these developments made the British more apprehensive and the Governor-General in Council ordered his officers to take strong action against the killers of Bhogchand and also against all those who disturbed the peace and who defied British authority in Naga Hills.[36] This led to two more expeditions into the Naga Hills under the command of Col. Vincent who, commanding a strong military force, camped at Mezoma. With a fully equipped army he attacked the strongest fort in the region at Khonoma.[37] But immediately after the expedition was over, he suggested to the British government to adopt a policy of non-intervention in the affairs of the Nagas.[38] The then Governor-General of India, Lord Dalhousie, approved the policy of non-intervention as proposed by Col. Vincent but he laid down in his despatch that the British Government should enter into trading so long as they corresponded peacefully, However, in case of a breach of peace, they should be ignored. To quote Dalhousie:

> "For these reasons I think that the advance post should withdraw now, at the time of our success and when we have exected all we threatened. Hereafter we should continue ourselves to our own gound protected as it can and must be protected; not meddle in the feuds and fights of savages; encourage trade with them as long as they are peaceful towards us; rigidly exclude them from all communication either to sell what they have got, or

---

36. *Ibid*.
37. All records agree that Khonoma fort was the most important fort in this region in terms of fighting equipment and military men. It was not only due to military strength alone that the British took over the fort, but also because some of the Nagas supported the British interference in the Naga Hills. See illustration of Khonoma fort on page 118 of this thesis.
38. A Mackenzie, *op.cit.*, pp. 113-114.

> **buy what they want to if they should become turbulent or troublesome."[39]**

This non-intervention policy of the British did not affect the nature and position of the Naga tribes, particularly the Angamis. In the 1860's when the Angamis were attacked by Manipuris, the British found their last opportunity of demonstrating their might and despite repeated pleas for help against the Manipuris, the British turned a deaf ear to the request of the Angamis. This attitude of the British made the Angamis more aggressive, but before the British could change minds with regard to this policy of non-intervention they setted some Kuki tribes between their territory and the hills controlled by the Angamis.[40] Possibly the British felt apprehensive of the Angami raids on British possessions, because the Angami Nagas who were the most prominent tribe and were in control of a large area of Naga Hills, raided the British subjects in South Cachar. This action of the Angamis forced the British to abandon their policy of non-intervention.[41] Besides, the British had almost exhausted all their diplomatic tactics and even their befriending policy did not help them. It is important to note

---

39. *Ibid.*, p. 114.
10. It may be noted that the British used the Kukis as a buffer, thus making the Kukis the traditional enemies of the Nagas for many years. This enmity lasted into the 20th century until the *Semoma* clan of Khonoma made a peace treaty with the *Thado* clan of the Kukis after which relations became friendlier. In the written record on the subject there is no trace of this peace treaty, but it has been derived from oral sources by the scholar. The scholar met many members of the Thado clan in December 1985 and also examined members of the *Semoma* clan in Khonoma for this information.
41. There is evidence to show that such raids over Cachar were a usual phenomenon even before the British. But this time the raids seem to have been more vigorously carried out due to the enmity with the British.

that when some of the Angamis were enlisted in the British force, which was a comparatively lucrative as well as relatively respectable job, the majority of the Angamis were least attracted by such incentives and preferred to remain completely self-reliant. Mackenzie observes:

> "They suggested also the enlistment in the military police. This last idea had also been tried without much success. The hillmen could not be induced to remain long under discipline; of 37 Angami recruits, the average proved to be only eight months."[42]

When Sir Cecil Beadon became the Lieutenant Governor, he recommended strongly the policy of force with regard to Anglo-Naga relations.[43] But there was a great delay in finding a solution to the problem because the British civil and military servants could not come to a common understanding. However, the major policies suggested by Sir Cecil Beadon in 1862 were as follows:

1. We might abandon North Cachar and all the hill tracts inhabited by the Nagas, and strictly enforce the Non-Intervention Policy of 1851.
2. We might advance to the hills, place special officers in charge, and maintain them by force of arms.
3. We might, while confining ourselves to the plains, cultivate political relations with the neighbouring clans and bring their chiefs into stipendiary police relations to ourselves.[44]

Out of all these suggestions, the one relating to abandoning North Cachar and all the hill tracts inhabited by the Nagas was not welcomed at all by the British

---

42. *Ibid.*, pp. 115-116.
43. *Ibid.*
44. *Ibid.*, p. 117.

Government. The reasoning here was that the abandoning of these areas in this manner would have appeared a kind of weakness on the part of the British and might encourage other indigenous groups in Assam and neighbouring areas to rally their forces and overthrow the British or at least stage a protest against the British Dominion.[45] This is well attested by the argument of Mackenzie,

> "The practical effect of such a measure would be that in course of a few years, Assam would be divided amongst the Bhutias, Abors, Nagas, Garos, Mishmis and other wild tribes; for exposed as Assam is on every side, if petty outrages were to be followed by withdrawal of our frontier, we should very speedily find ourselves driven out of the province."[46]

As a precautionary measure, some survey operations with regard to border settlement with Manipur were carried out. Col. Johnstone, without seeking the views of his superiors with regard to future policy, took two Angami villages of Medziphema and Sithekiema under British protection.[47] The British government at the top had not directed Col. Johnstone to advance beyond, the Assam territory but Johnstone did it as is obvious from his own statement:

> "Before leaving Calcutta, the Foreign Secretary said to me emphatically, when I urged an extension of our sway- 'but those villages (the Angami Nagas) are not British Territory and we do not want to extent the red line'."[48]

But contrary to the instruction, Col. Johnstone's own view was that the gradual process of 'civilization' of the

---

45. *Ibid.*
46. *Ibid.*
47. J. Johnstone, *op.cit.*, pp. 38-40.
48. *Ibid.*, p. 39.

tribes was the only means which could bring a settled advantage for the British and peace to the unprotected Nagas.[49] However, these measures also did not register any progress. The British government at the top assessed the situation thoroughly and realized that the mission so far carried out was mainly devoted to the maintenance of their border security and not to the extension of their authority in the hills. The task of all the officials prior to 1877 had concentrated much on the interference in feuds concerning various tribes.

It was during the year 1877 that a thorough topographical examination of all the hills inhabited by the Nagas was made and Kohima was worked out to be the most suitable centre from the point of view of a British outpost.[50] But before the British authority took over Kohima, Mezoma and Khonoma villages were considered by the British to be a dangerous threat to the proposed British establishment at Kohima. So an expedition was led by Carnegy in 1877 against Mezoma which completely destroyed Mezoma village.

> "The village was accordingly attacked and carried by assault and the whole of it with the exception of three or

---

49. *Ibid.*, pp. 43-44.
    It is generally believed by the colonial historians that the British brought civilization to the tribes as is also clear from this statement of Col. Johnstone. But the gradual transformation into a detribalized structure is a process historically inevitable. However, the fact that the British helped in speeding up this process by allowing missionary activity cannot be dinied.
50. A Mackenzie, *op.cit.*, p. 132.
    Before selecting Kohima, the British established their outpost in Chumukedima (Samuguting) and later shifted to Wokha. But possibly Kohima being a centrally located place made the British to shift their headquarters there.

> four houses was burnt to the ground ... Mozemah Nagas, being without food and shelter, and village and all stores of grain having been destroyed, made overtures for peace."[51]

Here it appears that after the Mezoma expedition, the British authorities became more alert and began to understand the structural analysis of the indigenous in the hills. It was for the first time that they began to identify the various areas of the different tribes. Our argument is fully attested by the fact that immediately after the Mezoma expedition, Kohima was subjugated by the British without any serious opposition. This encouraged the British to increase the frequency of their visits to other areas of Naga Hills. Kohima was made the Headquarters of Naga Hills with a sub-centre at Wokha; a strong police force was posted in the interior; and a house tax of Rs. 2 was taken.[52] In fact, until the British occupation of Kohima, the Nagas seem to have been completely unaware of the nature of colonial culture that the British possessed everywhere they went.[53] Even the villages which surrendered during the occupation of Kohima did not know that the occupation of Kohima would make it a permanent British seat. But gradually when the British officials assumed their real colonial character and laid out their future schemes for collecting taxes from the villagers they realized how

51. *Ibid.*, p. 131.
52. Verrier Elwin, *Nagaland*, Shillong, 1963, p. 24.
53. The colonial ambition of the British did not permit them to recognize men as human beings but rather as merely the objects of labour. Even in the nineteenth century the Bida State of South African tribes was ruthlessly exploited in the same manner as the Nagas. Michael Mason, "Production, Penetration and Political Formation—the Bida State 1859-1901" in *Modes of Production in Agrica, op.cit.*, pp. 205-224.

seriously it was going to affect the indigenous social organization which was fully managed and controlled by the chiefs, clans elders, and villages councils. This brings into focus what Johnstone implied by "civilizing tribes".[54]

However, the Angamis from Kohima also tried to work out some strategies to protect their indigenous organizational pattern. But the British, ambitious in their scheme of collecting levies, extended their net beyond Kohima to other villages. When the people of Khonoma came to know of this, they immediately thought of strongly resisting the British. It is interesting to observe how some Angamis followed their indigenous tactics in order to annihilate the British from the occupied hills. But apart from being too late for such offences, it was also impossible for the Angamis to hold out very long against the superior might of the British.[55]

But one cannot dismiss so easily the account of Angami resistance. The study of almost half a century from 1832 to 1880 shows how the Angamis, so small in manpower and materials, did not permit the British to gain a permanent foothold in the Naga Hills. Despite the best efforts of the British, the Nagas could not be so easily defeated. What then was the exceptional quality possessed by the Angamis that proved so tough for the British to subdue?

---

54. It is a pity that even after taking over most of Asia as their colonies, the British continued to indulge in the exaction of taxes in such areas where the indigenous people had to spend all their energies for eking out the barest sustenance. It was not the insignia of their political continuity but a means to maintain themselves, sometimes even without the legal sanctions of the state.
55. Even at such a critical hour, we find some cases of the killing of British civil servants by the Angamis. Such incidents were isolated and cannot serve much purpose except to illustrate that the Angamis were not ready to surrender to the British until the end.

We find that the Angamis were basically courageous, firmly determined and well-organized. From the beginning of the encounters with the Angamis, the British were apprehensive of the race. Damant's impression of Angami Nagas reads:

> "This tribe, *i.e.*, the Angami Nagas, the most war-like and probably the most numerous of all the Naga tribes with which we are acquainted occupies the centre of the great range of hills which divide Assam and Manipur... They are a fine set of men, very war-like and enterprising, taking freely to trade, and possessing in themselves the material for forming a fine nation: but they are bloodthirsty to a great degree, village fighting against village, clan against clan, and in fiercer quarrels sparing neither age nor sex."[56]

They would draw strength and inspiration from their ritualistic past as well on such occasions. Here the incident that precipitated the famous Battle of Khonoma (1879) is significant to record. By now the clans of Khonoma were well aware of the defeat of their neighbouring villages. The people Khonoma had been planning to send back the 'White Man' to his own country but they were also aware of the strength of the British. At this critical hour, *Thepfuchasa* of Khonoma killed a tiger.[57] This was followed by an elaborate ritual involving all the village warriors in a war dance exhibiting their weapons including firearms. Interestingly enough, to their own surprise, they found out that the village was in the possession of 95 muskets.[58] The discovery of this

---

56. G.A. Grierson, *op.cit.*, (Damant's Notes), p. 245.
57. According to Angami mythology, the tiger, God and man were brothers having the same mother. Therefore killing a tiger was like killing a man. The killing of a tiger was celebrated by elaborate dances and rituals. Petenihu Chase (50), of Khonoma village provided the details of the legends.
58. Sievizo Seyie (75), of Socunoma village gave this information.

fact and the realization of their strength gave them much courage. It was soon after that the people of Khonoma decided that they would send the 'White Men' back to where they belonged once and for all.[59] The people of Khonoma were determined to defend their land.

This patriotism is reflected in the songs and ballads composed during this period. A song composed by Yani-ü during the Anglo-Angami war clearly indicates the love the people had for their land. A loose translation of the song is as follows:

They came unnumbered and frearless
We knew them not but they wanted our land
Across strange fields and alien waters they came
Looking more like ghosts than man
Weilding their man-made weapons
and toyed at war, at war.

Lo! my homeland, my own
The Great God alone comes before thee
They neighbours lie crushed and captive
Oh send thy bravest, thy choiciest warriors
And early turn the While Man back.

Lay down thy dead and mourn no more
For we are proud and we are mighty
And our harvest turns gold beneath the skies
May we never know plague and hunger
May we vanquish those who would bleed our land
May our people then rise up in glory
And return to where life is good.[60]

---

59. In the meetings of the clans, fiery and patriotic speeches were made to arouse the feelings of the people. They shouted, "Shall we be ruled by strangers who dress like women?" *Ibid.*

60. Translated by Easterine Iralu. See appendix for the original text.

It was at this juncture that the British Political agent, G.H. Damant, who sought to impose British authority by forcing collection of taxes, became the victim of Khonoma.[61] Even the regiment escorting Damant comprising of 80 persons including military and police suffered a toll of 35 killed on the spot and 19 wounded.[52] The ones who survived faced great difficulty by managed to escape secretly to Kohima and deliver the news of Damant's death. This created a great sensation among all the British outposts located in the entire North Eastern region. They sent out messages to Shillong, Dibrugarh, Sibsagar and other places for mustering their forces and decided to launch a final attack on Khonoma.[63] But the killing of Damant and his men had encouraged the Angamis to a great extent and they had decided to immediately attack the British stockade at Kohima.[64] However, it took almost fortnight's time from Damant's death for both the hostile parties to have an open

---

61. Some historians, particularly the ones who wrote from the colonial point of view, have referred to Damant's death as 'murder'and have demonstrated Damant's visit to Khonoma as a friendly gesture, emphasizing that the visit had no ulterior intentions. But historically it is difficult to view Damant as a man ignoring his loyalty to his government. Damant himself wrote, "I would demand revenue from Khonoma and Jotsoma in the coming cold weather and in case of refusal realize it by force of arms; I believe the struggle must come sooner or later and it is to the interest of the whole district that the matter should not be deferred."
    H.K. Barpujari, *op.cit.*, Vol. I, p. 53.
    See also *Foreign Political Proceedings*, March, 1880, Nos. 331-395, India Office Library, London, K W No. 2, para 21.
62. *Foreign Political Proceedings*, February, 1880, Nos. 249-252, India Office Library, London.
    Cawley, "Siege of Kohima, 1979" in V. Elwin, *Nagas in the Nineteenth Century*, *op.cit.*, pp. 563-564.
63. J. Johnstone, *op.cit.*, pp. 147-160.
64. *Ibid.*

confrontation, "Khonoma, being sure of their early victory over the garrison, busied themselves on the 15th in burying their dead, feasting and rejoicing, and dividing their spoils, they delayed their attack."[65]

It was only on the 23rd October 1879 that the Khonoma warriors along with those from many other villages reached Kohima and surrounded the British stockade in an exceedingly planned manner, and were able to cut the British forces down to size. As recorded by Cawley:

> "The Nagas advanced slowly and surely, trenching as they advanced. They did this so cleverly, erecting barricades from the trenches, that they never exposed themselves in the least. It was like an invisible, but by no means noiseless, enemy creeping on step by step. The howls and war cries of thousands of Nagas who surrounded the stockade were truly awful and were not without their effect on the enfeeble grarrison."[66]

Looking into all the available literature on Naga warriorship, one could well assume the success of the angamis at this juncture. Even the derogatory shouting of Naga to the British just outside the stockade in Kohima makes it clear to what extent the Angamis had succeeded in their mission before the arrival of fresh troops from Manipur. Cawley has recorded the words shouted in derision by the Angamis to the British,

> "We (English) had come here and occupied lands, we had cut their trees, bamboos and grass. We wanted revenue from them and made them coolies... what will happen now."[67]

---

65. H.K. Barpujari, *op.cit.*, Vol III, p. 56.
66. Cawley, "The Siege of Kohima 1879", *op.cit.*, p. 576.
67. H.K. Barpujari, *op.cit.*, p. 54.

The Assistant Political Officer, also recorded that "at that time there were at least 4000 men surrounding us and of that about 300 had guns... the whole country was rising to annihilate us."[68] It was not the people from Khonoma alone, but Viswema, Ciedema, Jakhama, Jotsoma and Tsutuonoma *khel* of Kohima who joined hands to overthrow the British.[69] As Barpujari wrote,

> "To the Nagas it was a war of liberation against the English who had advanced into the heart of their territory, meddled into their inter-tribal feuds, subjected them the taxation and forced labour so hateful to them."[70]

It was the seige of Kohima that united many Naga villages against a common enemy. But at the eleventh hour the British troops, 2000 in number, under the command of Col. Johnstone arrived from Manipur and altered the whole situation. "The Nagas dispersed and the garrion was releived."[71]

Before we proceed further to give a detailed account of the most historic and final battle-"the severest fighting ever known on these hills", it becomes pertinent to enquire into the root causes which added a unique importance to the Angami village of Kohima before the entire colonial

---

68. *Foreign Political Proceedings - A*, February, 1880, No. 330, Cawley to Johnstone, V. Elwin, *op.cit.*
69. H.K. Barpujari, *op.cit.*, p. 57.
70. *Ibid.*
71. *Ibid.*, p. 58.
Among the various groups employed in the British army, we find the Nepalis taking a serious interest in all their efforts to help the British. Apart From joining the British army, they worked as coolies and servants from Manipur, it was the Nepalis who hurriedly carried the message from Hinde to Johnstone. The others who joined the British army were Manipuris, Kukis, Kacharis, Assamese and Garos.

schemes.[72] The British colonial masters extended their colonial net in Africa, Pacific Islands and Asia. The scrutiny of all the available literature on the nature of subjugation of indigenous and non-indigenous areas makes it sufficiently clear that it was these "savage tribes" whom the British found to be one of the toughest combatants upto the last moment of their surrender.[73] It is true that on the North Western Frontier, the Afghans proved no less significant in exhausting British might, though sometimes with Russian help. It is also true that the British had a very tough time fighting against the Zulus in South Africa, but then the Zulus were a much larger force to contend with in terms of number.[74] But the case of the Angamis retains its own specificity and uniqueness in the history of British colonialism. J.P. Mills the former Deputy Commissioner of Naga Hills (1935-37) wrote,

> "The rising of 1879 was the last effort by the Angami Nagas to drive from the hills the hated British invader. Of this tribe, the men of Khonoma, a big village of some five hundred houses, are second to none in their physique and intelligence. When we first came into touch with them they had long been irresistable in war and from time immemorial had claimed the right to take tribute and heads from the feeble Kacha Naga villages of the North Cachar Hills. So stiff was the resistance put up that it took more than forty years to finally bring the Angamis into subjection. Between 1835 and 1850 ten military

---

72. A. Mackenzie, *op.cit.*, p. 137.
73. J. Johnstone, *op.cit.*
74. The Zulu tribe were the most powerful in Africa. In 1879, the Zulus attacked a British camp and slaughtered 1600 men, half of them British. But ultimately, in the final analysis, they were not able to hold out against the superior might of the British.
    A.W. Palmer, *A Penguin Dictionary of Modern History*, Middlesex, 1962, p. 363.

> expeditions had to be made into the hills. In the later year Khonoma was taken by assult of troops supported by artillery. The policy of non-interference was then tried with the result that twenty two raids were reported within the next years. A string of frontier posts in the North Cachar Hills was then tried but this, in turn, proved equally ineffective."[75]

Another piece of evidence to this effect in provided by Col. Johnstone, who actually participated in the war.

> "It was the misfortune of those in the Naga Hills expedition, that they were overshadowed, and their gallant deeds almost ignored by the Afghan War then in progress. Some of the English papers imagined that the operations in the Naga Hills were included in it, and Government of India, which has only eyes for the North West Frontier showed little desire to recognise the hard work amidst difficulties far greater than those which beset our troops in Afghanistan. The force engaged, hoped that the capture of Khonoma which was achieved after such hard fighting and at so great a loss, would have been at least recognized by some special decoration, but this hope was disappointed, apparently for no other reason, than that the troops engaged fought in the east and not in the west of India. Kaye, the historian, once said that 'the countries to the east of the Bay of Bengal were graves of fame.' Well did the Naga Hills campaign, prove the truth of his words. A bronze star was the reward of a bloodless march from Kabul to Kandahar, but not even a clasp could the spared to commemorate the capture of Khonoma, and those who never saw a shot fired, shared the medal awarded equally with those who fought and bled in the bloody fight."[76]

75. J.P. Mills, "Headhunting and Wars" in *Nagas in the Ninteenth Century*, edited by V. Elwin, *op.cit.*, pp. 564-565.
76. J.Johnstone, *op.cit.*, p. 181.

It was perhaps the only time in the entire colonial history that an army general was involed in fighting against a single village.[77] Not only a general but a number of other officers with 3000 soliers were involved in that "bloody fight" in order to capture a village with 500 houses. The Khonoma warriors definitely fought with the greatest determination to defend their land. J.B. Bhattacharjee writes:

> "The prolonged war of the resistance that the little known village of Khonoma in Nagaland offered to the military might of the arch imperialist of the west has earned its people an enviable position to all freedom loving peoples... the blood, sweet and tears of the people of Khonoma, the martyrdom of those who laid their lives, their sacrifice and suffering will continue to inspire our present and future generations with the spirit of patriotism and love for freedom."[78]

An understanding of the colonial history in the global context makes it clear that it was the advancement of China and Burma which added strategic significance to the Naga Hills apart from the importance in the British economy.[79] With all this in view, the killing of Damant seems to have served what Archduke Ferdinand's assassination proved for World War I. From the early 1930's the British had begun to pursue their policy in the Naga Hills with firm determination, but Damant's death just gave one excuse for the total destruction of the rising Angami influence in the Naga Hills.

There is no doubt that the spirit of oneness and nationalism had its birth due to the presence of the British.

---

77. Brig. General Nation was incharge of the Khonoma campaign.
78. J.B. Bhattacharjee, "Challenge of Khonoma", *Journal of Naga Research Council*, Kohima, 1987, Vol. 101, No. 1, pp. 18-22.
79. Nirode K. Barooah, *David Scot in North-East India*, Delhi, 1970.

Tajenba Ao aptly puts it:

> "The spirit of self rule was gaining momentum among the people of Khonoma by designing to overthrow the British administrators; the 'Chakka Fort' was the bed of patriotism that never could be assailed by any force. The influence of Khonoma diplomacy increased among Angami villages into a front of common alliance that the British could not overcome."[80]

Evidently, the Angami villages of Khonoma and Kohima figured prominently in the Anglo-Naga relations leading to the British colonization of the Naga Hills. The Angamis demonstrated their might particularly in preserving their indigenous socio-economic and politico-cultural system. It also focuses on the British design in taking over the Naga Hills—the process which took half a century.

By this time the French contact with China had also considerably improved. So there was no time but to muster whatever support and strength was available to the British from various areas for a final attack on Khonoma. The charge of affairs was under Brigadier-General Nation. He commanded the forces brought from Assam. Manipur and other areas of the North Eastern region. Finally, Khonoma was defeated and its:

> "wonderful terraced cultivation confiscated and its clan dispersed among other villages. The result was that the dispossessed villagers found themselves not only deprived of their homes, but confiscated of their setted cultivations. They were during a whole year reduced to the condition of homeless wanderers, dependant to a great extent on the charity of their neighbours and living in temporary huts in the jungles. The result was widespread sickness and mortality."[81]

---

80. Tajenba Ao, *A History of Anglo-Naga Affairs*, Mokokchung, 1959, p. 21.
81. Verrier Elwin, *Nagaland, op.cit.*, p. 22.

But in spite of the defeat and the ghastly treatment by the British which followed, Khonoma survived, and the true heritage of Khonoma was well expressed by J.P. Mills:

> "Severe punishment was meted out and Khonoma was razed to the ground and its inhabitants dispersed. It now flourishes as old, however, the sword has been exchanged for the pen and parties now go forth to seek rupees instead of heads. From Khonoma has come the first Naga magistrate, and its enterprising black-kilted traders travel as far as Bombay and Rangoon. But old customs are still kept and old songs sung and tales told. The best of her old spirit remains and Khonoma, mindful of her generations of unquestioned power, shows no signs of becoming a decadent, pseudo-civilized nonentity, ashamed of its past and uncertain of its future."[82]

It is of great interest and importance to note that a hundred years after the war, on the 22nd November, 1979, the people of Khonoma celebrated the 'Centinnial Commemoration of our Heroes' with the same spirit of patriotism and freedom. On that day they wrote of their warriors who died in the battle-

> "It is one hundred years now since they fell. But they are not forgotten. Their names are still remembered and cherished, and their deeds talking about and sung in ballads. They died but they did not die in vain. Their courage, their patriotism and their sense of honour have always been a source of inspiration to our people and will continue to be for generations yet to come... this is also an occasion where we should honour our heroes by trying to imbibe their spirit—the spirit of the heroes who made the supreme sacrifice in the defending our fatherland and our honour, the heroes who died so that we might be free."[83]

---

82. J.P. Mills, *op.cit.*, p. 565.
83. Quoted from the booklet, *Centinnial Commemoration of Our Heroes*, Khonoma, 22nd November, 1979.

Looking into the resources of the Naga Hills, one feels convinced that the subjection of Naga Hills was more important to the British from the strategic point of view, than the dominant interest in British colonialism of extracting revenue, draining away the raw materials and marketing the goods, although it is true that a number of tea gardens were transferred from Naga Hills to Assam. Peace with the Angamis was well seen by the British long before the final occupation as a major solution to the problems of this region. From the post-occupation phase of Kohima and Khonoma, it is obvious that the British felt that their authority could be well maintained in the Naga Hills by controlling the 'turbulent Angamis'. However, the whole epoch of colonization did not pass without bloodshed on both sides. Though the Angamis fought with all possible course and means, it was historically impossible for them to resist the British colonization which had by then enveloped the whole Asia, with the result that by the 1880's, the British had firmly extended and entrenched their colonial domination into the Naga Hills.

6

MODERNIZATION AND ITS IMPACT

In the previous chapters our analysis has focused on those developments which transferred the political control of the Angami possession from indigenous to colonial hands. To safeguard their colonial interests in India, the British found it necessary to control the territories of the North Eastern Frontier. The occupation of these areas not only provided them with the natural resources of tea, oil, minerals and forest products, but also adequately equipped their efforts in the expansionist design. On this North Eastern Frontier, the Naga Hills occupied a prominent position. However, as we have already dealt with this aspect in the precious chapter, we shall look into those processes which transformed the Angami society into a modernized one.[1] A

---

1. The studies devoted to the nature of various indigenous societies of the world have recorded the clear demarcation of various phases of transition and the process involved therein. But in the case of the Angami Nagas, the transition appears to be a prolonged one. This cannot be merely attributed to their isolation from the rest of the world but also to the inherent strength of the race people which sustained this prolonged transition. For studying this transitional phase, the Sage Series on African modernization and development has developed a perspective which will certainly prove rewarding for studying all indigenous societies.
   See *Modes of Production in Africa,* Vol. 5, edited by D. Crummey and C.C. Stewart, London, 1981.

careful study of all the mechanisms, changes and forces which were involved in this process of transition shall figure in this chapter. Since the study is devoted to the two villages of Kohima and Khonoma, the main centres of the Angami Nagas, the pivotal focus shall be on the development taking place in them. However, the influences which this process of development worked over the entire Naga society cannot be ignored altogether.

Generally our sources illustrate that the transition from the traditional to contemporary society was accompanied by various forces of confrontation and conflict.[2] When we deploy the principle of historical materialism, one finds that this transition from pre-modern to modern was always historically inevitable. But this historical inevitability forms the critical link in these two phases (pre-modern and modern) which was further strengthened by the British occupation of the area.[3] It has become necessary for the British to have a complete political control over every part of the Indian subcontinent to project their colonial dominion and when they discovered India's indispensability for their colonial ends,

---

2. The Angami society was tempted by the manifestations of colonial culture on the one hand, but was keen to preserve their autonomy, social organization and indigenous culture on the other. This has been the case with many indigenous societies in the world.
   Bogumil Jewsiewicki, "Lineage Mode of Production, Social Inequalities in Equatorial Central Africa", in D. Crummey and C.C. Stewart, *op.cit.*, pp. 70-93.
   Steven Feierman, *The Shamba Kingdom*, Wisconsin, 1974.
3. Prior to the British appearance, the Angamis had already established contact with the Indians in terms of the exchange of goods. But with the British occupation their mobility increased tremendously because the construction of new roads and other means of communication was the first thing the British took over to strengthen their foothold. Robert Reid, *op.cit.*

they gradually tried to erode its territorial and political structure, in which, of course, India's own weakness made no less a significant contribution.[4] However, the increasing efforts in the expansionist design brought them into conflict with other nations in the world apart from the smaller communities which initially were not prepared to part with their system. In this connection, Naga Hills was no exception to the rule. The annexation of the Naga Hills meant the control of the entire North Eastern Frontier and the protection of their interests in Burma and China.[5]

It was not only by force that the British succeeded in subduing the Angami Nagas, but their powers of persuasion, their sense of duty, religion and other welfare activities made their task easier.[6] The Angamis until then had not been exposed to the temptations of material culture

4. K.K. Datta, *Survey of Indian Social Life and Economic Conditions in the Eighteenth Century*, 1707-1813, Calcutta, 1961.
S. Chandra, *Parties and Politics at the Mughal Court*, Aligarh, 1959.
Although the process of deterioration had set in much earlier, after the collapse of the Mughal Empire, the infighting among various regional kingdoms and the subsequent exploitation of the Indian masses weakened the personality, laying the ground for transfer of political power to the British.
5. Nari Rustomji, *Imperilled Frontiers*, Delhi, 1983.
6. Other than political agents, the contribution of the American Baptist missionaries with medical facilities and other welfare activities also worked as a potential mechanism in bringing the Angamis under British authority because the Angamis at that stage did not make the distinction between British and American interests but saw them both as one race—the 'White Man'. The trust that the missionaries instilled in them was therefore transferred to the British as well. At this juncture, there were also two contradictory forces at work. On one hand, the British trying to develop some kind of a centralized system for subjecting all the Nagas and on the other hand, the Nagas trying to preserve their indigenous autonomy.

which the Burmese and the Indians had experienced for centuries under various changing dynasties and maharajas.[7] The societies in India has started stratifying intensely on caste and religious lines from ages past. The communal ownership of means of production had long since disappeared in India.[8] The other socio-religious mechanism of Buddhism, Hinduism, Islam and Sikhism had established new trends in an organized form of worship with its complicated set of rituals, in some cases dehumanising man. The rulers would indulge in religious conversion of their subjects to create a mass base for their persistence of kingly institutions.[9] But the Naga areas were unfamiliar with all these material manifestations. They still retained in their clans the chiefs as heads of their communities and managed their affairs on communal lines.[10] The indigenous organization had its own socio-cultural past, hence this nature of Angami society proved a great advantage to the British in building up their base in Angami area. Among the various operative forces which

---

7. The Angami society had a peculiar nature. It did not enjoy the status conferred on most such frontier tribes by intra- border trade which could help the growth of transition even without its own agrarian or other economy.
8. R.S. Sharma, *Material Culture and Social Formation*, *op.cit.*, pp. 8-19. D.D. Kosambi, *The Culture and Civilization in Ancient India*, Delhi, 1977, pp. 96-108.
9. Religion was used as an ideological mechanism from early ages. To obtain the mass base the kings fostered conversion from Hinduism to Buddhism, Islam or Sikhism. All these measures changed the conditions of the people. Thomas Arnold, *Preaching of Islam*, London, 1896.
10. Since the Angami society remained untouched and uninfluenced by Brahmanical and Buddhist rituals, varna orientation or by the Islamic tenents, the society was fertile for work of the Christian missionaries.

penetrated the North Eastern region with the British entrance, ecclesiology has played a very important role in the entire process of the modernization of the Angamis.[11] To quote Terhuja:

> "If one responsible dynamic factor were to be singled out for an overall change in the life of the Nagas, it would undoubtedly be the introduction of Christianity among them."[12]

Here we can compare without any doubt the Naga conversion to what Arnold Toynbee said about the English conversion from the religion of the so-called Heroic Age to Christianity:

> "The conversion which was really the beginning of all things in English history, was the direct antithesis of that; it was an act which merged half a dozen isolated communities of the barbarians in the common weal of a nascent western society."[13]

Likewise, the various groups of Naga tribes were integrated into a common religion without distressing their distinct identity.

The British military expedition in this area and missionary activities commenced almost simultaneously. In 1832, the first military expedition to Naga Hills was undertaken and the first band of missionaries made their appearance in the area in 1836.[14] In the beginning the attitude of the Angamis towards the missionaries was very

---

11. *Ibid.*
    F.S. Downs, *Christianity in North East India*, Delhi, 1983.
12. Khrieleno Terhuja, "The Christian Church Among Angami Nagas", in *Tribal Situation in India*, Vol.13, edited by K.S. Singh, Simla, 1972, p. 294.
13. Arnold Toynbee, *A Study of History*, Vol. I, London, 1983 (reprint), p. 19.
14. Frederick S. Downs, *op.cit.*, p. 33.

hostile. Those who consciously or unconsciously got converted to Christianity were persecuted or excommunicated by their Angami brethren from their clan or village.[15]

Before we proceed further to a detailed description of missionary activity in this area, there emerge some important questions:

(*i*) What interests did the American Baptists have at a time when the colonial expansion was carried out by the British who were mostly Anglican, Methodist or Presbyterian?

(*ii*) How were the two able to ex-exist in their missions–the British with their colonial cause and the Baptists with their missionary zeal?

However, these questions can only be resolved by observing the materials available to us. The sources reveal that there were instances of the British officials coming into conflict with the advancing missionaries. "There was never the close personal relationship between missionaries and British officers in Naga Hills."[16] But it was the American Baptists who made a lasting impact on the Angami mind because even after the departure of the British and the coming of other denominations to the Naga Hills, the Angamis seems to have remained uninfluenced and are predominantly Baptist Christians even today.[17] Initially,

---

15. This persecution of the Christian converts by their Angami clansman continued even until the 1950's. The scholar has interviewed many early converts who suffered after embracing their new faith, as well as with staunch traditional animists who took part in the persecution.
M. Horam, "The Advent of Christianity and its impacts on the Naga Society", Unpublished paper.
16. Frederick S. Downs, *op.cit.*, p. 34.
17. 64 per cent of the population of Nagaland are Baptists. Joseph Puthenpurakal, *op.cit.*, p. 1.

however, the process of conversion was very slow.[18] The first missionary to the Angamis, Rev. C.D. King, entered Angami territory in 1879 and started his mission in Kohima in 1881.[19] But it was only after five years of dedicated effort that the fruit of his labour was finally realized in the first Angami convert, *Lhousietsu*, of Kohima village, in 1885.[20] It was possibly the presence of certain British civil servants who did not get along with the missionaries that slowed the process of conversion to some extent. In addition, it appears that the Angamis by nature are more conservative and resistant to change than the other Naga tribes which further slowed down this process.[21] But then the march of time waits for none and the activities of the missionaries were not merely confined to conversion. Christianity was for that matter a most organized and reasonable religion and it carried in its wake other social activities and benefits as well. In such remote areas the combination of medical care and education coupled with teachings of morality and fellow–feelings could not be ignored. It was a time when other countries of the world particularly in Europe were making great advances in science, technology and particularly in education which taught people to reason and overcome traditional prejudices.[22] It was due to the

18. B.C. Allen, "District Gazetteer of Naga Hills (1905)" in *The Imperial Gazetteer of India*, Vol. XVIII, Delhi, p. 287. See also K. Terhuja, *op.cit.*, p. 295.
19. Keviyiekielie Linyu, *The Angami Church Since 1950*, Bangalore, 1983, pp. 40-41.
20. *Ibid.* Kohima Field Baptist Centenary Jubilee Souvenir, edited by K. K. Peseyie, Kohima, 1935, p. 8.
21. Keviyiekielie Linyu, *op.cit.*, p. 41.
22. This was the age of the Industrial Revolution in Europe where fresh waves of thought and religious reformation accompanied the intense scientific and intellectual activity generated during this period. J. Hexter and Richard Pipes, *Europe Since 1500*, New York, 1971, pp. 738-777.

process of this christianization that the traditional and vague animistic beliefs gradually started eroding in society. When the concept of one God and Christ being the only Son of God was taught to the Nagas who believe in a number of spirits and have an accompanying set of elaborate rituals, they responded to the simplicity and logicity of the new religion. Christianity ushered in a transformation from animistic traditions based on superstitious practices to a more orderly society where the guiding principle was no longer that of natural human urges but based rather on the laws of God and love for one's fellow man. A reverence for such a vague host of spirits was a waste of time for a man who had to struggle painfully in the effort of living, and it also conditioned his outlook due to superstitious limitations. We can well say that the conversion provided institutionalized religion where man was side by side taught the rudiments of morality and also ensured his emotional security in the community. The so–called glory that the Angamis derived by hunting the heads of their fellow men was replaced by a cause for the service of humanity.[23] The usual sacrifice of animals and other resources such as grains and other necessities of life were a waste and could neither fetch peace for the departed soul nor bring home a sense of reason. Apart from this there are numberless intricacies and extravaganzas which form part of the animistic faith in the earlier period. For instance, a funeral involved a great number of intricate rituals and sacrifices which were time consuming as well as expensive and often proved to be an unnecessary burden to the family. The amount of restrictions for the children and female members of the society including restrictions of certain

---

23. Frederick S. Downs, *op.cit.*
See also *Khonoma Diamond Jubilee Booklet*, February 4-6, 1972.

foods caused nothing but a sense of inferiority. This discrimination extended also to exclusion from specified meetings and gatherings. These taboos not only restricted the participation of women but also hampered seriously the growth of social progress and culture. Besides fostering a sense of subordination among equal human beings, it also compartmentalized the clans and villages and merely perpetuated the intra–clan and intra-village rivalries. Such frequent in–fighting would constantly divert the attention of the clans from building up an agrarian economy and served to accentuate the neglect of the exploitation of the forest and other economic resources which would otherwise have been an immense help in the overall community development. The amount of labour which was utilized for months in intra–clan warfare was a serious loss to the whole community particularly when there was no other form of labour made use of. This would consequently lead people to live by plunder and make warfare endemic to Angami polity.

In course of time, missionaries with their firm determination operated carefully taking note of all such problems. Initially they opened up the facilities for educating the Angamis and stressed medical care but the Anglo–Naga struggle which lasted for half a century did not permit the Baptists to register any appreciable progress until the twentieth century.[24] However, during this period, the foundation was laid among many other Naga tribes, and other tribes in Assam. These efforts directly influenced the people

24. From 1832 to 1880 expeditions were sent to the Naga Hills to subdue the Nagas. Though the missionaries were at work during the same period, the constant resistance of the Nagas did not help the missions to establish themselves firmly. However, the mission did not give in and continued even during the period of crisis. See the Chapter on Colonization of this thesis.

of the North East region. It was during this period that the other denominations and schools of Christian thought made great progress in this region.[25] All these developmental activities of the missionaries associated with the religious cause left a deep impression on Naga society. It seems that though the missionary activities were now and then discouraged by the British colonial servants, their influence continued to grow beyond measure. We find that during the last days of the British rule and only a decade after they left that the number of Angami Christians rose tremendously. In 1885, there was only one Angami who was baptized.[26] By 1936 there were 1,534 baptized members.[27] Church membership rose from 2,882 in 1955 to 11,000 members in 1981.[28] This increase cannot be characterized as sudden in nature but was the result of long and painful efforts carried out by the Baptist Mission in Nagaland in general and Angami area in particular. The Angamis certainly noticed the changes for the better which the Baptists had brought by taking care of the tribe.[29] The general education of the people at the hands of the missionaries opened up the eyes of the Angamis to a new world. The initial indifference towards Christianity would

---

25. The other tribes such as the *Garos, Khasis* and *Mizos* were also converted during this period.
    Frederick S. Downs, *op.cit*.
26. Keviyiekielie Linyu, *op.cit.*, p. 41.
27. K. Terhuja, *op.cit.*, p. 294.
28. Keviyiekielie Linyu, *op.cit.*, Chart No. 2.
    However, the rest of Nagaland experienced a much faster growth rate in church membership ... "The Church grew fast with more than 10,000 adult baptisms a year, mostly of young tribal people, until Nagaland held the highest ratio of regular worshipping Christians to population of any state in the world." John Pollock, *Billy Graham, Evangelist to the world*, New York, 1979, p. 4.
29. The first Angami convert received tutelage under the missionaries paving the way for the benefits of education to the whole tribe.

not have been present due to a desire for preservation of identity alone but also because of a suspicion of British colonial policy. When the Angamis realized that the Baptists had no motive other than to render service to humanity in the name of God, they voluntarily offered themselves as converts to the new faith. One can well imagine how the Angamis have been drawn towards this plain religion of the Baptists which not only liquidated all the outdated taboos in Angami society but also trained them in the new path of progress. Horam worte:

> "The constant feuds and head-hunting of these people were cut short by the new doctrine based on love and brotherhood. Apart from this , The Naga literature before the coming of Christianity was purely oral, now they have been written..."[30]

The education of the tribe which forms one of the major themes of the process of conversion laid down the basis for all future developments. It was as a result of education that the Angamis began to differentiate their past and future and chose to advance their careers in various branches of learning. The technical education opened up many opportunities for the Angamis. One may note here that some of the first Angami educated persons who obtained college degrees chose to be pastors and church workers not necessarily because all of them were overwhelmed by evangelism alone, but because they could foresee also that the only way to awaken their fellow men was to devote full attention to their education and development through the facilities provided by the missionaries.[31] Here it will not be wrong to say that C. D. King was the father of this process

---

30. M. Horam, "The Advent of Christianity and its Impact on Naga Society", *op.cit.*

of modernization. He was the first missionary to the Angamis and started a school which was followed up by his successors, although with great difficulties in the beginning:

> "With the departure of C.D. King at the beginning of 1887, the small primary school he started in 1882 became extinct. It was revived by Rivenburg in 1889. It continued upto 1895 with some forty-six students on the roll.[32]

Thus the seed of modern education was sowed by C D King and Rivenburg but the real pioneers in Angami education were the Supplees:

> "The Supplees who were first designated for Impur station, were transferred to Kohima in December 1922 to take charge of school work especially in view of Rivenburg's retirement. By that time, the need for a full fledged high school in the Naga Hills for the Naga boys and girls was strongly felt among hill missionaries like Pettigrew, Grozier, Longwell, Tanquist and Baily. So, the Supplees began answering their need to the best of their ability. Four years after the arrival, a grant of Rs. 2000 was secured for the school from the missionary union. In 1925, class seven was opened and again class eight followed in 1926.[33]

Apart from this High School the missionaries encouraged higher education. *Khosa* and *Sevilie* were sent to Dibrugarh to study medicine in 1913 and 1914 respectively.[34] Likewise, *Hucha Savino* became the first

---

31. Nisier Meru is an example of a case where he left his job in the Police Department to become an evangelist working with Dr. Rivenburg in the Kohima Mission. *Khonoma Diamond Jubilee Booklet, op.cit.*, p. 8.
32. Joseph Puthenpurakal, *op.cit.* p. 121.
33. *Ibid.*, p. 122.

Angami Veterinary doctor in 1917.[35] The advancement of medical education also certainly increased the life span and decreased the morality rate. In such remote areas the Angamis were naturally prone to many kinds of natural diseases which could not be cured in those days. The dependence on herbs and other indigenous types of remedies was not always reliable in early times. The growth of educational institutions increased the mobility of the Angamis and brought them into constant touch not only with Indians but also with some Europeans during the first world war.[36] This exposure created an impact on their minds especially in relation to their awareness of their own emerging identity. To quote Asoso Yonuo, they saw :

> **"How the great civilized nations fought for their ends and interests while Nagas were condemned as barbarious for their headhunting wars."[37]**

Their European experience fostered a new sense of unity and oneness:

> **"Far from home the Naga soldiers from different villages and communities came together for comfort, and thus developed a comradery which transcended age-old prejudices and separatism...It may be said that on the battlefields of France and in the trenches the iron spearhead of a new Naga nationalism was forged."[38]**

---

34. Based on field work. The scholar has personally interviewed *Dr. Savilie Iralu* to get this information.
35. *Khonoma Diamond Jubilee Booklet, op.cit.*, p. 21.
36. There were a good number of Angamis who went to Europe during this war. *Khosa* was one of them.
37. Asoso Yonuo, *op.cit.*, p. 125.
38. Colin Johnson, "The Naga Dilemma", in *The Naga Nation and its Struggle,* edited by Teresa Aparicio and Jorgen B. Jorgensen, Copenhagen, 1986, p. 17.

After acquiring a good education, a number of Angamis entered the Civil Service in the British India Government. *Mr. A. Kevichusa* became the first Naga graduate in 1924 and went on to became a Deputy Commissioner.[39] Entering these various professions not only provided an impetus to shift to the new religious outlook and impressed the need of education for all gave them employment opportunities to supplement their resources from agriculture. This exposure to the outside world broadened their outlook and they carried new ideas of developing their cultivation, various arts and crafts and exploitation of the forest resources. Obviously the economic development within the Angami society expanded the social division of labour and stengthened further the entire indigenous organization of settled agricultural villages. Side by side, the efforts to enhance the opportunities of carrying out trade with distant areas and the importing of various articles of daily use also improved. It was only after the British occupation that the scope of trade and commerce expanded and extended even beyond the international borders. Krusietso was the first merchant who visited some South East Asian countries for trade purposes in the beginning of the twentieth century.

This information was given to the author by his daughter Tuno (95), still living in Kohima. The increase of mobility of Angami society together with the efforts of the British administration led to the construction of roads and tried to link up various areas in Naga Hills. All these measures monetized the economy and now the commodities could not only be exchanged for other commodities but gradually for money. Developing road

---

39. The scholar has conducted personal interviews with *Mr. Kevichusa* for this information.

systems made it easy to carry goods over long distances. This improvement in communication and the growing economy led to an increase in population.[40]

All these developments were gradually consciously or unconsciously introducing changes which modernized the entire Naga society. Not only were the institutionalized from the religion, the efforts of education, the economic developments, but the social organizations also gradually emerged into a new form and pattern. The way of life that the Angami were exposed to at the hands of the missionaries—the nature of dress, the changes in the institution of marriage, the social coordination, and other new festivities—completed the transitional phase. By the time the British colonial masters were departing, the Baptists had tremendously contributed to this process of modernization in the shape of all the aforesaid developments. Khrieleno Terhuja puts it:

> "The church has oriented the Nagas to a wider fellowship of humanity and the treasure of modernity. The church must be rooted in its concerned cultural setting to provide intelligent interpretation of the Christian faith and a proper relationship with new trends in Society.[41]

This process of modernization can partly be attributed to the British particularly during the period from 1880-1947. Since the British had realized from the very beginning that the Angamis could not be controlled by force, but persuaded by a friendly attitude, they took interest in developments affecting the Angamis.

---

40. The population of Kohima District was 57,672 in 1901, it rose 108, 924 in 1961. The Angami population in 1961 was 33, 687. Hamlet Bareh, *Nagaland District Gazetteers, Kohima*, Kohima, 1970, p. 57.
41. Khrieleno Terhuja, *op.cit.* p. 301.

The construction of roads and the introduction of educated Nagas into the new administration proved a great help to the Angamis. They took a lot of interest in improving the economy of the area because the persistence of poverty and backwardness meant a loss of revenue for the British as well. Though the British administrators were gradually detribalizing the Angamis, so far as the administrative system was concerned, it did not affect seriously the traditional ways of administration and supervision at the village level. The village elders continued to be powerful in taking major decisions on important matters even down to the present day. In fact, the British officials often complained against the missionaries and emphasized that the latter were destroying the culture of the Angamis by restricting the participation in festival dances and by prohibiting the drinking of *zu*, the rice wine.[42] But it is irrational to believe that the Angami life and culture would have remained static without the influence of the missionaries. The missionaries did make a lot of mistakes at the initial stage,[43] but they also restricted certain practices in Angami culture which had become outdated and merely contributed to social waste. For example, the missionaries were very much against the practice of headhunting and animal sacrifice and other superstitious practices.[44]

From the above discussion, it becomes clear that it was the activities of the missionaries and the British stay in the area which laid the foundation of this process of

---

42. J.P. Mills, *The Ao Nagas, op.cit.*
43. The mistakes they made were due to a lack of distinction between religion and culture–there was a wholesale condemnation on their part of anything indigenous.
44. Joseph Puthenpurakal, *op.cit.*

moderization. By the time both the parties left Naga Hills, the Angamis had reached a stage of self-reliance and the economy had grown slightly above subsistence level. It can be termed as self-sufficient in the sense that the Angami society was not much dependent on import of food and most items of its consumption were produced locally. However, the departure of the European community opened a most important era in the history of the whole Naga society.

Since the colonial exploitation had reached a level where it was becoming increasingly difficult for the Indians to tolerate, the aspirations of people—the idea to drive out the British from India—gathered momentum from the beginning of the twentieth century.[45] Amidst these developments, the Nagas became aware of their identity and their historical roots and had decided to settle their own political future. They formed the Naga Club in 1928.[46] Though the Club was initially a social and cultural forum, the development taking place in other parts of India vis-a-vis British rule forced the Club to look into the political problems of the Nagas arising out of the British departure from India. It needs to be stressed that before the arrival of the British the Nagas were politically independent. They did not share any of the governmental systems of India or Burma. It was purely a non-state society with peculiar polity where society functioned in a pure democratic form. John Butler, *op.cit.* It is very clear that the Naga Hills had been brought under their control by the British out of sheer political and strategic need and it was necessary for the safety of the British colonial empire from

45. J. Nehru, *Unity of India*, London, 1948.
Jim Masselos, *Indian Nationalism*, Delhi, 1985, pp. 199-224.
46. V.K. Nuh, *Nagaland Church and Politics*, Kohima, 1986, p. 81.

the North Eastern side. Obviously, there did not prevail much of exploitation of the Nagas under the British if we look at the problem from an economic point of view.

The material level of the Nagas was very low when the British entered. There was not much produce to reduce the hardship of life. They had no proper means of communication and transport. It was with the coming of the British that some roads were constructed for the British. That some Nagas got employment opportunities though on a very small level is also obvious. Hence the harsh existence of life had been reduced by the British to some extent. Besides, the British did not detribalize the internal social organization, nor did they interfere with the internal affairs of the people. These measures had created a good image of the British in the Angami mind which persists to the present day. As a result, the Nagas made it clear that once the British left India, they would like to be left undisturbed politically as they were before.[47]

When talks for independence were going on in India, the British set up a commission in 1927 under Sir John Simon to study the working of the administration in india.[48] This Commission, popularly known as the Simon Commission, visited India in 1929 together with Clement Attlee and E. Cadogan as members.[49] The Naga Club submitted a Memorandum to the Simon Commission when they visited Kohima in which they clearly stated that they should be left alone to determine their own future the day the British left the Naga Hills. The memorandum states:

---

47. At the time when the British were leaving India, the seeds of political consciousness had already sown in the Naga mind. A spirit of nationalism was growing among them.
48. M. Alemchiba, *op.cit.*, p. 163.
49. *Report of Indian Statutory Commission*, Vol. I, India Office Library, London, 1930, p. 75.

"We, the undersigned Nagas of the Club at Kohima, who are the only persons at present who can voice our people, have heard with great regret that our hills were included within the Reform Scheme of India without of our knowledge, but as the administration or our Hills continued to be in the hands of the British Officers we did not consider it necessary to raise any protest in the past. Now, we learn that you have come to India as Representatives of the British Government to enquire into the working of the system of government and the growth of education and we beg to submit below, our view with the prayer that our Hills may be withdrawn from the Reform Scheme and placed outside the reforms but directly under the British Government. We never asked for any reforms and we do not wish for any reforms.

Before the British Government conquered our country in 1897-1880 we were living in a state of intermittent warfare with the Assamese of the Assam valley to the North and West of our country and Manipuris to the South. They never conquered us, nor were we ever subjected to their rule. On the other hand, we were always a terror to these people. Our country within the administered area consists of more than eight tribes, quite different from one another with language which cannot be understood by each other, and there are more tribes outside the administered area which are not known at present . We have no unity among us and it is only the British Government that is holding us together now.

Our education at present is poor. The occupation of our country by the British Government being so recent as 1880 we have no chance or opportunity to improve in education and though we can boast of two or three graduates of an Indian university in our country, we have not got one yet who is able to represent all our different tribes or master our languages much less one to represent us in any council of a Province. Moreover, our population is very small in comparison with the population of the plain districts in the province, and any representation that may be allotted to us in the council will have no weight whatsoever.

Our language is quite different from thóse of the plains and we have no social afffinities with Hindus or Mussalmans. We are looked upon by the one for our beef and the other for our pork and by both for our want of education which is not due to any fault of ours.

Our country is poor and is does not pay for its administration. Therefore, if it is continued to be placed under the Reform Scheme, we are afraid that new and heavy taxes will have to be imposed on us and when we cannot pay them all our lands will have to be sold and in the long run as we shall have no share in the land of our birth, and life will not be worth living then. Though our land at present is within the British territory, Government has always recognised our private rights in it but if we are forced to enter the council all these rights may be extinguished by the unsympathetic Council, the majority of which number is sure to belong to the districts. We also much fear the introduction of foreign laws and customs to supercede our own customary laws which we now enjoy.

For the above reasons, we pray that the British Government will continue to safeguard our rights against all encroachments from other people who are more advanced than us by withdrawing our country from the Reform Scheme and placing it directly under its own protection. If the British Government, however, wants to throw us away, we pray that we should not be thrust to the mercy of the people who could never subjugate us, but to leave us alone to determine for ourselves as in ancient times. We claim to represent all those tribes to which we belong: Angamis, Kacha Nagas, Kukis, Semas, Lothas and Rengmas."[50]

---

50. V.K. Nuh, *op.cit.*, p. 81-83.

In 1945, the Naga Hills Districts Tribal Council was formed by C.R. Pawsey, the Deputy Commissioner of Naga Hills, with the aim of uniting the various Naga tribes. Its existence, however, was short-lived. A conference of the representatives of various tribes was held in 1946 where its name was changed to that of the Naga National Council (NNC) which ultimately emerged as the only political organization in the Naga Hills, and later, under the leadership of Mr. A.Z. Phizo, an Angami of Khonoma, assumed a militant nature.[51] The NNC embarked upon negotiations with the government regarding the future of the Nagas. Sir Akbar Hydari, the then Governor of Assam undertook negotiations with the Nagas on behalf of the Indian Government.[52] As a result of the meetings, a Nine Point Agreement was entered upon. However, the clause dealing with the 'period of Agreement' became a bone of contention as each party had its own interpretation [53]

In the mean time, the spirit of nationalism through the inspiration of the Naga National Council was spreading like wildfire throughout the Naga Hills. These developments posed a serious problem for the Indian leaders. Here it is essential to observe, before demonstrating the nature of modernisation, a dialogue which took place between the Naga leaders and Mahatma Gandhi. In July, 1947, A.Z. Phizo

---

51. Asoso Yonuo, *op.cit.*, pp. 160-224.
52. *Ibid* .
53. The Clause reads as follows:
"The Governor of Assam as the Agent of the Government of India will have a special responsibility for a period of ten years to ensure the due observance of this agreement; at the end of this period, the Naga National Council will be asked whether they require the above agreement to be extended for further period or a new agreement regarding the further of the Naga people arrived at." M. Horam, *op.cit.*, p. 142.

with a Naga delegation met Mahatma Gandhi and revealed the political situation in Naga Hills. They stressed that the Nagas were going to be independent after the British departure. On this, Gandhi said to the Naga leaders:

> "We do not want the British. And they are going. If you say that you are not Indians and your country does not belong to India then the matter must end there. Nobody will force you to join the Indian Union."[54]

And when the Nagas told him that they were going to declare independence on 15th August, he said to them,

"Why wait August 15? Why not declare it today"?[55] The Nagas also told Mahatma Gandhi that India was going to attack the Nagas when she became independent Gandhi's reaction was:

> "Don't you trust me? She has no right to do so. If force were to be used then I will sacrifice my life for you and I will ask them to kill me first before a Naga is shot."[56]

From this dialogue, it becomes clear that nothing was settled in black and white. The Gandhian philosophical attitude which must have been more dominated by the crisis that the country had been facing in other parts of India, did not solve the Naga problem to any degree. However, the Nagas took Gandhi's words in good faith and returned to Nagaland. On their return they declared their Independence from the British on August 14th, 1947, with great celebration and a telegram was sent to the United Nations.[57]

---

54. A.Z. Phizo's letter to Mr. Rajiv Gandhi, Prime Minister of India, dated May 10th, 1986.
    Mr. A.Z. Phizo told the details of his meeting with Gandhi to the scholar in his home in London in January, 1985.
55. *Ibid.*
56. *Ibid.*
57. Asoso Yonuo, *op.cit.*

Why such developments took place is an important question which we shall try to examine at this stage. Here we should not forget that the Nagas are a Mongoloid race who had nothing in common with the Dravidian or the Aryan culture. After settling in the Naga Hills they lived for a long time with their independent socio-political set-up. Ever since the Nagas settled in the Naga Hills their history has been greatly influenced by outsiders, but the Nagas were never subjugated by foreign powers and they developed a great value of freedom and democracy. Andrew Gray, the British scholar wrote,

> "Naga history has been framed by relationships with foreign power... but the Nagas were never conquered and deprived of their independence which was dispersed through village self government.[58]

On one hand, the Nagas remained isolated and had very little contact with the outside world and on the other hand, in spite of their isolation they remained in touch with some of the developments taking place in Assam and Manipur. They had seen the fate of the tribes like the *Boros, Ahoms,* and *Maiteis,* and realized how the process of Brahmanization had imposed the rigid caste structure on them and liquidated their identity which the Nagas were not prepared to risk. As Frederick Downs wrote :

> "... that christianity and the process of modernization closely associated with it became a means whereby many of the hill tribals sought to preserve their identity in the face of the perceived threat of assimilation into the Hindu society of the plains."[59]

---

58. A Gray, "The British in Nagaland—the Anthropology and their Legacy" in *Naga Nation and its Struggle,* Edited by Teresa Aparicio, Copenhagen, 1986, p. 38.
59. Frederick S.Downs, *op.cit.*, p. 8.

Another factor that traumatically affected the transition of Naga society into modernization was the Second World War when the Japanese and the British fought the bloodiest battle in Kohima in the heart of Angami country. According to Asoso Yonuo,

> "It was the Second World War which had propelled psychological cataclysm far beyond its confines than anything that had taken place during the British rule for about seventy years. Thus the war also enshrined powerful political commotion, dissension and ferment among the educated middle class Nagas, particularly those of the areas affected by the war."[60]

According to Admiral Lord Mountbatten:

> "The Battle of Kohima will probably go down as one of the greatest battles in history."[61]

The views of Field Marshal Wavell on the same battle reads:

> "When the history of the war comes to be written, the fight here will be put down as one of the turning points of the war... when the Japanese were routed and their downfall really began."[62]

As a result of this war, the Nagas suffered extremely. But on the other hand, some Nagas bagged the advantages which had a serious impact on their society. The sudden war time construction activity, posting military supplies and other necessities pumped a lot of money into Naga hills. This brought into being a rich class of contractors thus creating a neo-rich class in Naga society.

---

60. Asoso Yonuo, *op.cit.*, p. 150.
61. Arthur Swinson, *Kohima*, London, 1966, p. xiii.
62. *Ibid.*

It is as a result of their independent historical past that the Nagas did not join the Indian Independence Movement. Instead the NNC declared their own independence a day before India did. The NNC began to organize the Naga tribal groups into an organized state. But a few years after India's independence, Indian armed forces moved into Nagaland in a bid to integrate the Nagas into the Indian Union by force—the most unfortunate policy that has ever been followed in Indian history. Since the Army has its own way of doing things, particularly in an area which is totally new to them, mass scale destruction took place. Villages were burnt and people forced into camps where the women and the children received the worst of the treatment. Many died in starvation. In the jungle people were forced to exist on roots, insects, and other forest products. The suffering and disruption was more than the Nagas had faced in the Second World War when the Japanese invaded India through Naga Hills.[63]

During this crisis a group representing a large proportion of the population who wanted independence went underground. Taking advantage of the situation, some of the petty government officials along with some Naga opportunists formed the Naga people's Convention (NPC) and opened a dialogue with the Indian Government. The outcome of the meeting between Nehru and the NPC resulted in the creation of Nagaland state without consulting the Naga people.[64]

---

63. Information regarding this period of hostilities between the Nagas and the Indian Army is based on personal field work. See also *Nagaland File*, edited by Luithui and Nadita Haskar, Delhi, 1984.
64. M. Alemchiba, *op.cit.*, p. 186. When the NPC delegation returned to Nagaland after signing the Sixteen Point Agreement with the Indian Government conferring statehood to Nagaland within the Indian Union, there was a widespread protest against the Agreement which culminated in the assassination of the President of the NPC.

After the creation of the state, a new phase of development on Nagaland commenced on two levels—the government level and the private or individual level. Huge amounts of funds were pumped into the state for the purpose of development.[65] A lot of these resources got concentrated into Kohima, which is the capital of the state and which had been a central place from its very inception. However, this sudden flow of easy money had grave repercussions on the Angami society. The officials who were responsible for handling these sums of money became corrupted as they succumbed to the temptation of quick wealth. This corruption became, in a sense, a way of life as there was no accountability for these funds. New industrial establishments were formed and the extension of bureaucracy following statehood created new employment facilities. The plans for education, social welfare and medical facilities improved. Side by side, the influx of Marwaris and non-local business communities with their stalls and godowns in Dimapur also spread to other areas, reaping the advantage of this fresh frontier of economic enterprise. The growth of transport, communication and other construction activities were carried out. All this resulted in giving of permits for various enterprises and industries. The setting up of colleges, schools, social welfare institutions and even a university greatly changed the social structure. Rail communication and air services made it easy for the Angamis to venture more freely into travel to other states and countries.

All these changes had accentuated the formation of a *nouveau riche* class. The net result of the process of modernization particularly after statehood was the emergence of an

---

65. These funds were not only used for development, but also served the subtle tactical purpose of subverting feelings of nationalism by eroding the moral fibre of the society.

uneven social structure. Because all these developments did not effect much change at the grass root level, it was only the small part of urban population which benefitted from these developments and emerged as a new middle class. The progress of trade and commerce and the nature of political activities were mainly responsible for the emergence of the bourgeoisie and this provided them the initial capital to invest further the multiplication of their resources through business, transport or construction works.

The impact of these developments on the two villages of Kohima and Khonoma were historically unavoidable because of their location. Kohima, being the capital of Nagaland, received more than its due for developmental activities. The new capital enabled the people from various urban and rural areas to settle down here.[66] This influx naturally resulted in an unprecedented rise in population and subsequently affected the land and market prices which shot up sky-high within a few years' time. This not only did away with the earlier method of land distribution but also brought into existence the peculiar methods of land-grabbing. For the merchants, Kohima was a paradise where contracts and concessions were easily awarded by politicians who could give licences and permissions for trade and commerce, and which also had a ready market for more expensive products.[67]

---

66. The population of Kohima district was 108,924 in 1961. In 1981, it rose to 250,105. Kohima town had a population of 67,216 in 1981. *Source: Statistical Handbook of Nagaland 1984*. Directorate of Economics and Statistics, Government of Nagaland, 1984.
67. From the very beginning the integration of Indian polity was eroded because of the election funds. The politicians were financed by the businessmen and when they assumed power they were forced to the demands of the businessmen and lost political autonomy, becoming tools in the hand of businessmen. Same tactics have operated in Nagaland in the post statehood phase.

Since the process had increased tremendously, some of the new rich went in for constructing houses for rent and hotels which provided temporary refuge for travellers both from rural as well as urban areas.

All these influences worked in different directions to change the Angami social formation. The emergence of social division of labour due to the increasing amount of trade and industry disturbed the rhythm of the Angami indigenous production relations in Kohima and Khonoma. This led to the intense social stratification based on material strength which was completely absent prior to this. The exploitation of the members of Angamis by their own men commenced speedily. Though the entire indigenous society of the Angamis has not been assimilated fully by this phenomenon into a complete transformed class society, the process has been set in motion by the growing trend of capitalism which has linked the entire society with the world capitalism in terms of trade and other influences.

The cultural level has been seriously affected. The superficial westernization in matters of dress, food habits, music and other activities became popular. These developments have seriously challenged the traditional way of life. For instance, taking the matter of a wedding among Angami, in earlier times, an Angami wedding was a simple affair. Festivities could be completed with the killing of one pig and a few chickens to feed the few guests. The whole ceremony was carried through with a minimam of fuss, especially regarding material arrangements. But the scene is much changed now. There is a great preoccupation with physical arrangements which tend towards the extravagant, sometimes involving even lakhs of rupees with the killing of a great number of mithuns, cows and pigs.

A drastic change that has taken place is in terms of

administrative organization. Prior to these developments, the Angami social organization in Kohima and Khonoma was under the Village Council and chiefs, who would look into the matter of conflicts and other problems in the clan or village. But the new imposed government has led to the erosion of the authority of the traditional Village Councils. Thus going to a modernized court for immediate solution to their problems regarding property or land disputes, clan feuds and other problems connected with day to day life saps the resources of the people. All these show that the process of modernization has been that of an uneven nature and a large section of Angami society has not been in a position to benefit from such developments. The heirarchical nature of society on economic lines is getting established very rigidly in an area which had hitherto escaped caste orientation but the fact cannot be denied that the entire Angami society is improving with all the attendant evils of modernization.

As we have seen in the foregoing discussion in this chapter, the Angami society has gone through different phases of transition—from pre-modern to modern. These changes have been a historical necessity. But it is an undeniable fact that the twentieth century has been a "period of rapid change such as humanity has probably never before experienced", as Hutton has so perceptively observed.[68] This traumatic period has left a deep emotional strain on the minds of the Angami Nagas. As the Naga philosopher, T. Sakhrie, makes us aware:

> "The Nagas made a leap, as it were, from a distant past into the glare of the present century... found their world greatly changed. They looked about with uncertainty and pinched themselves to be assured that all that was really

68. J.H. Hutton, *op.cit.*, p. xi.

true... people became suddenly restive with the existing state of affairs. There was social unrest, economic unrest, political unrest. Everywhere there were cries for better, bigger and nobler things. The era brought a new impetus to all fields of human endeavour.[69]

69. Verrier Elwin, *op.cit.*, p. 71-72.

7

CONCLUSION

The discussion in the foregoing chapters warrants the conclusion that the indigenous social formation of Khonoma and Kohima, was a succession of socio-economic formations, surpassing the earlier one in social, political, cultural and other spheres. However, what the analysis of the chosen aspects reflects in this study needs to be considered at greater length.

The waves of migration from western China and South East Asia to these hills were many and spread over a long period of time. These waves of migration were chiefly necessitated by the incompatibility that was rapidly developing due to shrinkage of resource potential and the population growth. These conditions were given further impetus by aggressive rulers. But before these tribes could complete their march to settle down in these hills which came to be named after them, they cut across different politico-cultural regions. However, that should not be seen as an ascent from one socio-economic formation to another. The Nagas passed through a complicated and protracted process of settlement. The Naga hills were not endowed with rich resources to attract the Angami particularly with such a geographical remoteness, but in this regard their history was determined by their own circumstances.

In fact the history of indigenous people all over world has clearly revealed that wherever they settled they perferred to remain isolated as far as they could from the relatively more developed societies. For all the mongoloid tribes who migrated to this area the climate and the terrain which seems to have played a significant role in their process of settlement in this region.

The Angami villages of Kohima and Khonoma in Naga hills had similar factors in their entire process of formation. In this entire process the role of productive forces was of course most crucial, but this fact need not be overstressed, for their spiritual, cultural and ethnic mechanisms had also run ahead of the development of productive forces in the establishment of these villages. In the pre-colonial phase they continued to lag behind in most spheres of political, social and economic life in the South East Asian context. But that did not prevent them from producing great warriors, craftsmen, agriculturists in such harsh and unsuitable terrain. The formation of these villages strengthened the Angami social organization and generated a cohesiveness and cooperation among its members to reproduce their relations of production with gradual improvements in hunting and agriculture, animal husbandry and craft-making. But the mode of appropriation continued to be communal in character and a dominant feature of Angami society. This did not usher in complete transformation of Angami society into a class society. Though the process of generating surplus was not completely absent, the channels through which it was extracted lay more on spiritual and cultural rather than on purely economic lines. The *Zievo* (priest) was the most important figure among the Angamis before the evolution of the institution of Angami *Peyumia* (chiefs) at the village level. The Zievos' demands, which were mostly on the pretext of pleasing deities through sacrifices and other rituals, were satisfied by the share from hunting, harvest and human labour. Since the *Zievo's* materialistic tendencies were limited because ultimately he was a part and parcel of the same village or clan, the extraction did not take place solely for economic purposses. It was as a result of this that most of the Angami *Zievo* did not get transformed into a political group and instead legitimized the position of the village chiefs when the transitional forces penetrated. Possibly this would have been one of the factors in prolonging transition. Lack of material forces also contributed to this slow transformation of the Angami society but the simultaneous existence of institution of priesthood and chiefs did play a greater role in the entire picture and the village formation continued to rest on its laurels. The other factor responsible for the slow transition was the slow growth of technology and other productive forces. The structural phenomenon of these villages revolved around the priesthood and village elders with a more democratic apparatus which alone possessed the political-judicial authority to settle the conflicts. In the pre-colonial period it is historically inconceivable to think of the Angami villages in the form of state at any level. The Angamis of Kohima and Khonoma did emerge powerful at times even to the extent of exercising their authority not only on Angami villages but stretching over to non-Angami Nagas as well, but this super-imposition cannot be translated into the existence of a full-fledged superstructural phenomenon. Though western scholars have formulated various theories with regard to state formation often widely testing the empirical situation of Africa, all these studies failed to persuade us in following any of them because the case of Angamis is a case of a purely non-state society with some elements necessarily involved in the tide of historial advance. These elements of cohesion before reaching a stage and assuming new dimensions were disrupted by the penetration of colonial forces. This suddenly arrested the developmental processes in that direction and super-imposed a new apparatus with two tendencies of persuasion and subjugation at the hands of Baptist missionaries and the British colonialists respectively.

This opened up an important and transitional phase in the entire history of Angami society. The Angamis fought all through to preserve their independence for almost half a century. The strength with which the Angamis countered the British has been recognised as unique by the British themselves in their history of colonization. In this struggle, the Angamis derived immense strength from their singular ethnicity and exhausted their potential in their attempt to stop the British from disrupting the rhythm of their indigenous social formation. The subjugation of the Angamis by force was much helped in its advance by the persuasive forces of the missionaries who sincerely carried out their programmes of economic welfare, medical care, education and religious activities. These developments were an entirement to the Angamis and were certainly not linked directly with attempts to control the Angami country. They did not represent the British colonialism but were purely American Baptists who made centres in the Angami villages of Kohima and Khonoma. This process led to an uneveness in social and economic affairs but did not delink the cultural values.

Advanced socio-economic formations do not class with the vital interests of the people and act for the development of new social relations as opposed to reactionary formations. It is interesting to note elements of both in the process following British intrusion. The imposition of the British political apparatus and the missionary culture which followed in its wake resulted in detribalization. The new Angami converts did away with much of the old religious traditions, some of which were now superfluous, but some of which are now seen to be an irreplaceable loss. Christianity could not cut across cultural barriers completely and could not delink some of the traditional practies, some of which continue even to this day as part of the indigenous past.

The colonial political structure which was a temporary phase because it was short lived did initiate the destruction of social organization to the extent of leaving it utterly powerless in its affairs in the long run. The British appointed their own officers to settle the affairs concerning Nagas in general and Angamis in particular. The creation of new Angami village chiefs (Gaon Bura) by them curbed their tendency to revolt. The succession of a chain of officials, the limitation of boundaries of the areas and other reform activities connected with the cultivable and non-cultivable land resulted in the dilution of a singular ethnic and tribal strength. Thus began the gradual process of class formations which were ultimately fostered by the process at the hands of independent India's central structure. When finally the British colonialism came to an end, their distinct ethnicity posed serious problems for the Indian government because the Angami voiced their feelings again with the rest of the Nagas for preservation of their independent political identity and for their past history. This struggle for independence continue still today. But a section has chosen to co-exist as a part of Independent India by accepting a state within India. However, events did not run that smoothly and many temptations were offered to the newly created state under various developmental programmes. Unfortunately the development continued on more uneven lines bringing in easy money to transform a few into the nouveau riche and the rest dependent on them for their daily bread. The growth of population was a simultaneous process which helped to intensify the social stratification of Naga society on class lines. Hence a non-state of Angamis got transformed and directly linked to the capitalism which gave room for much faster growth.

APPENDICES

APPENDIX-A

The original text of the prayer of the leader who first migrated to Khonoma. From page 95.

Phemeu Kepfu Die therieu

Themia Kelhu runa, kenei kevi runa, thepe-thero keju runa, chu terhu kevi runa puo pfuketuo su hakiha biamu; ha; ishu. Sitse puo zeko, 'O' idi puo ki vorlie.

APPENDIX-B

The original text of the prayer for the consecration of Khonoma village.

Phese ja

Terhomia kiju hakiha pie uya chupiezhu shie,
Hakiha lhou di keviu chu tuowe
nhicunomia bu tholi-khwutho va u pheluo kesou chubie tuowe
Nuopu nuolhou bu lhou kecauchu lhou runa hau souzie tuowe
Tieuzu liecu tuo kenei keviu chutuo
Chu-terhu nu kuokelie runa chutuowe
Thephou-thena chulielho
Runa hanu kelhouko bu lhou miathi-miagwu chu di keviu chu tuowe.
"Uwe".

APPENDIX-C

A folk song composed by Saruu of Gariphe village during Khonoma-Gariphema war. Page 116.

Garipheju

Garipheju Terhuso upfu
Saruu no Khwunoria kevo
Apfu Pelhu anie Pukahie
Pedo huro kethu tuo cau
Noru pedo aru thukhono
Japfu phiki nie kewheko ze
Terho michu juu gei keza
A whoru mu kolie sho dinu
Pecu ru mu perie tsu yieho.

APPENDIX-D

The original text of a folk song composed by Yani-u during Anglo-Angami war. Page 145.

Khwunomia Geizo

We lu kiju sikemo kunu
Thernia mou terhomia kemhie
Mero we chu seirhi pekrei pie
Puorienosho nha mezu no ze
Sono perhie vor ubarie
Bieu imu lapezei lielo
Kiju chaju lugei kebie ha
Terhomia sie ukeno phelie
Kha miatsuhie uraju khrisa
Uramia we vi sono zhazie
Themia rei lhu tierei zurei ni
Chu metsie chu uramia pelo
Zosie derei uthino zhavi
Mhie medohie thethse theyu chu
Thepe thero uramia terhie
Chadu haze sikemoku vo
Uru-u su uzhalho-u chu
Uro peko uru-u whogei
Pezilie di lolalie yagwe.

BIBLIOGRAPHY

Primary Source

Allen, B.C., *Naga Hills and Manipur,* Calcutta, 1905.

——, "District Gazetteer of Naga Hills (1905)", in *The Imperial Gazetteer of India,* Vol. XVIII, Delhi, 1905.

Ao, M. Alemchiba, *A Brief Historical Account of Nagaland,* Kohima, 1970.

Ao, Tajenba, *A History of Anglo-Naga Affairs,* Mokokchung, 1959.

Barpujari, H.K., *Political History of Assam (1826-1919),* Vol.I, Gauhati, 1977.

——, *Problem of the Hill Tribes: North East Frontier,* Gauhati, 1981.

Barua, Hem, *The Red River and Blue Hills,* Gauhati, 1954.

Barua, K. L., *Early History of Kamrupa,* Gauhati, 1966.

Bhuyan, S.K., *Studies in the History of Assam,* Gauhati, 1965.

——, *Atan Borgohain and his Times,* Gauhati, 1965.

Bowers, Ursula Graham, *Naga Path,* London, 1950.

Butler, John, *Travels and Adventures in the Province of Assam,* Delhi, 1885.

Chatterjee, S.K., *The Place of Assam in the History and Civilization of India,* Gauhati, 1955.

Das, N.K., "Land Management, Dual Inheritance and Redistribution Among the Zouno-Keyhouno Naga", in *Agrarian Situation in India,* Vol. I., Calcutta, 1982.

Devi, Lakshmi., *Ahom Tribal Relations,* Gauhati, 1968.

Downs, Frederick S., *Christianity in North East India,* Delhi, 1983.

Elwin, V., *Nagaland,* Shillong, 1963.

——, *Nagas in the Nineteenth Century,* Bombay, 1969.

Furer-Haimendorf, C. von, "Nagas" in *The Illustrated Encyclopedia of Mankind,* Vol.II, London, 1978.

Gait, E.A., *A History of Assam,* Calcutta, 1967 (reprint).

Ganguli, Milada, *A Pilgrimage to the Nagas,* Delhi, 1984.

Gogoi, P., The Tai and the Tai Kingdom, Gauhati, 1968.

Gray, Andrew, "The British in Nagaland—the Anthropology and their Legacy" in *Naga Nation and its Struggle,* edited by Teresa Aparicio and Jorgen B. Jorgensen, Copenhagen, 1986.

Grierson, G. A., *Linguistic Survey of India,* Vol. III, Part II, Varanasi, 1903.

Haskar, Nandita and Luithui, *Nagaland File,* Delhi, 1984.

Hodson, T.C., *The Naga Tribes of Manipur,* London, 1911.

Horam , M., *Naga Polity,* Delhi, 1975.

Hunter, W.W., *A Statistical Account of Assam,* in two volumes, Delhi, 1975 (reprint).

Hutton, J.H., *The Angami Nagas,* London, 1921.

——, *The Sema Nagas,* London, 1921.

Johnson, Colin, "Naga Dilemma" in *The Naga Nation and its Struggle,* edited by Teresa Aparicio and Jorgen B. Jorgensen Copenhagen, 1986.

Johnston, James, *Manipur and the Naga Hills,* Delhi, 1971 (reprint).

Jacobs, Julian, *The Nagas,* Thames and Hudson, London, 1990.

Keviselie, *Arbervirolas Naga Mussihkka,* Tromso, 1985.

Linyu, Keviyiekielie., The Angami Church Since 1950, Bangalore, 1983.

Mackenzie, Alexander, *A History of the Relations of Government with the Hill Tribes of North East Frontier of Bengal,* Calcutta, 1884.

Mills, J.P., *The Lhota Nagas,* London, 1922.

——, *Rengma Nagas,* London, 1937.

——, "Headhunting and Wars", in *Nagas in the Nineteenth Century,* edited by V. Elwin, Bombay, 1969.

——, *The Ao Nagas,* London, 1973 (reprint).

Nath, R. M., *The Background of Assamese Culture,* Shillong, 1949.

Nuh, V. K., *Nagaland Church and Politics,* Kohima, 1986.

Pollock, John, *Billy Graham- Evangelist to the World,* New York, 1979.

Puthenpurakal, Joseph, *Baptisty Missions in Nagaland,* Shillong, 1984.

Reid, Rober, *History of Frontier Areas Bordering on Assam,* Delhi, 1942.

Rustomji, Nari, *Imperilled Frontiers,* Delhi, 1983.

Sanyu, Visier, "The Intra-clan equation in the village formation process in Early Angami Society–A Case Study of Khonoma Village", *North-East India History Association Proceedings, (Pasighat), 1986.*

Shurhozelie, "Tenyidie Seminar Va Diau", *Ura Dze,* edited by Beilieu, Kohima, 1974.

——, *A Ra Kezivi,* Kohima, 1984.

Smith, W.C., *The Ao Naga Tribe of Assam,* London, 1925.

Swinson, Arthur, *Kohima,* London, 1966.

Terhuja, Khrieleno. "The Christian Church Among Angami Nagas", in *Tribal Situation in India*, Vol. 13, edited by K. S. Singh, Simla, 1972.

Watters, Thomas, *On Yuan Chwang's Travels in India (A.D. 629-645)*, London, 1904.

Yonuo, Asoso, *The Rising Nagas*, Delhi, 1974.

Secondary Source

Abeles, Mark, "In Search of Monarch: Introduction of State Among Gamo of Ethiopia" in *Modes of Production in Africa*, 12 Vol., edited by D. Crummey and C.C. Stewart, 12 Vols., Vol. 5, London, 1981.

Allen, Charles, *A Mountain in Tibet*, London, 1983.

Anderson, Perry, *Passages from Antiquity to Feudalism*, London, 1974 (reprint).

Arnold, Thomas, *Preaching of Islam*, London, 1896.

Bareh, Hamlet, *History and Culture of Khasi People*, Shillong, 1964.

——, *Nagaland District Gazetteer, Kohima*, Kohima, 1970.

Barooah, Nirode K., *David Scot in North-East India*, Delhi, 1970.

Bernal, J. B., *Science in History*, 3 Vols. London, 1965.

Bhattacharjee, J. B., "The Eastern Himalayan Trade of Assam in the Colonial Period", *North East India History Association, First Session Proceedings*, Shillong, 1980.

——, "State Formation in Pre–Colonial Tribal Northeast: A Case Study of the Dimas State", *The North–Eastern Hill University Journal of Social Sciences and Humanities* vol. II, No.4, July-September, 1984.

——, "Challenge of Khonoma", in *Journal of Naga Research Council*, Vol. 101, No. 1, Kohima, 1987.

Bible, The Book of Judges.

Buchanan, Keith, *The South East Asia World*, London, 1967.

Chandra, C., *Parties and Politics of the Mughal Court*, Aligarh, 1959.

Claessen, Henri J. M., "The Internal Dynamics of the Early State" in *Current Anthropology*, Vol. 25, No. 4, August-October, 1984.

Claessen, Henri J. M. and Skalnick, Peter (ed.), *The Early State*, The Hague, 1978.

Cressey, George B., *Asia's Land and Peoples*, New York, 1963.

Crummey, D. and Stewart, C.C. (ed.), *Modes of Production in Africa*, Vol. 5, London, 1981.

Datta, K. K., *Survey of Indian Social Life and Economic Conditions in the Eighteenth Century, 1707-1813*, Calcutta, 1961.

Drew, F., *The Northern Barrier of India*, London, 1877.

Edward, Herbert B. and Herman, M., *Life, of Sir Henry Lawrence*, London, 1873 (reprint).
Engels, Friedrich *The Origin of the Family, Private Property and the State*, London, 1972 (reprint).
Fairbank, John K.; Reischauer, Edwin O. and Craig, Albert M., *East Asia Tradition and Transformation*, London, 1973.
Fazl, Abul, *Akbarnama* (Persian (1601), English Translation by Agha Ahmad Ali and Abdul Rahim, Calcutta, 1864.
Feierman, Steven, *The Shamba Kingdom*, Wisconsin, 1974.
Fitz Gerald, C. P., *A Concise Histroy of East Asia*, London, 1966.
——, *The Southern Expansion of the Chinese People*, London, 1972.
Gibbs, M., *Feudal Order*, London, 1949.
Gordon, P.R.T., *The Khasis*, Calcutta, 1914.
Hall, D.E.G., *A History of South East Asia*, London, 1958.
Hangloo R.L., *Situating Medieval Indian State*, Delhi, 1995
——, *Agrarian System of Kashmir*, (1846-89) Delhi, 1995.
Hexter, J. and Pipes, Richard, *Europe Since 1500*, New York, 1971.
Hindess, Barry and Hirst, Paul Q., *Pre-Capitalist Mode of Production*, London, 1975.
Jewsiewick, Bogunil, "Lineage Mode of Production, Social Inequalities in Equatorial Central Africa", in *Modes of Production in South Africa*, edited by D. Crummey and C.C. Stewart, London, 1981.
Jordan, Robert Paul, *National Geographic*, Vol. 171, No. 5, May, 1987.
Kosambi, D. D., *The Culture and Civilization in Ancient India*, Delhi, 1977.
Laibman, David, "Modes of Production and Theories of Transition" in *Science and Society*, Vol. XLVIII, No. 3, Fall 1984, New York.
Majumdar, R. C., *British Paramountcy and Indian Renaissance*, Vol. IX, Part I, Bombay, 1970.
——, *Ancient India*, Delhi, 1971 (6th Revised Edition).
Marshall, S. D., "Political Power and the Economy in Primitive Society", in *Essays in Science of Culture in Honour of Leslie A. White*, edited by E. Dole and R. L. Carniero, New York, 1960.
Mason, Michael, "Production, Penetration and Political Formation – The Bida State 1859-1901", in *Modes of Production in Africa*, edited by D. Crummey and C. C. Stewart, 12 Vols., Vol. 5, London, 1981.
Masselos, Jim, *Indian Nationalism*, Delhi, 1985.
Mc Crindle, J. W., *Ancient India as Described by Megasthenes*, edited by R. C. Jain, Delhi, 1972.
Momjan ,Kh., *Landmarks in History*, Moscow, 1979.
Morgan, Lewis H., *Ancient Society*, London, 1877.

Mukherjee, R., *The Rise and Fall of East India Company*, Bombay, 1973 (First Indian Edition).

Nehru, J., *Unity of India*, London, 1948.

Ptolemy, Claudius, *Geographia VIII*.

Sardesai, D. R., *South East Asia – Past and Present*, Delhi, 1981.

Sharma, R. S., *Indian Feudalism*, Delhi, 1965.

——, *Material Culture and Social Formation in Ancient India*, Delhi, 1983.

Sharma, S. N., *The Neo–Vaishnavaite Movement and the Satra Institution of Assam*, Gauhati, 1966.

Sinha, Surajit, "State Formation and Rajput Myth in Tribal Central India", in *Man in India*, Vol. 42, No. 1, January-March, 1962.

Sladkovsky, M. I., *The Long Road: Sino–Russian Economic Contracts from Ancient Times to 1917*, Moscow, 1981.

Thapar, Romila, *From Lineage to State*, Bombay, 1984.

Thompson, E. A., *The Barbarian Kingdom in Gaul and Spain*, Medieval Studies, Vol. VIII, Nottingham; 1963.

Toynbee, Arnold, *A Study of History*, Vol. I, London, 1983 (reprint).

Vansina, Jan, *Kingdoms of the Savanna*, Wisconsin, 1975 (reprint).

——, *Oral Tradition as History*, Wisconsin, 1985.

Watson, William, *China Before the Hand Dynasty*, London, 1961.

Wolf, Eric, *Peasants*, London, 1966.

Yadav, B.N.S., *Society and Culture in Northern India*, Allahabad, 1977.

Index

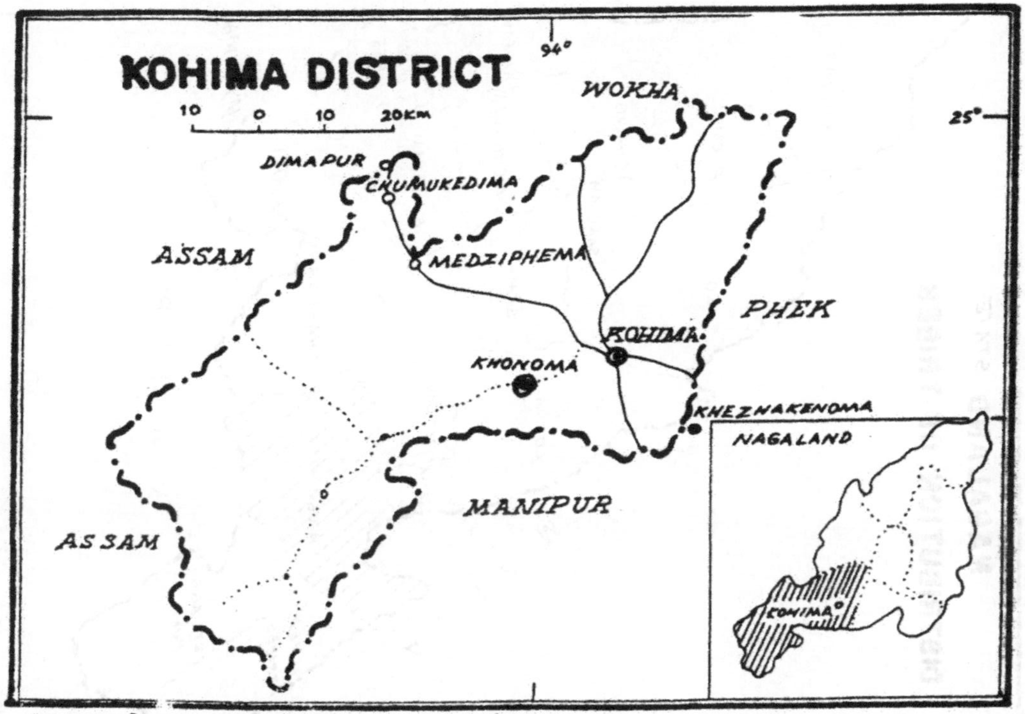

Source:- Directorate General, Survey of India, 1981

Fig. 1

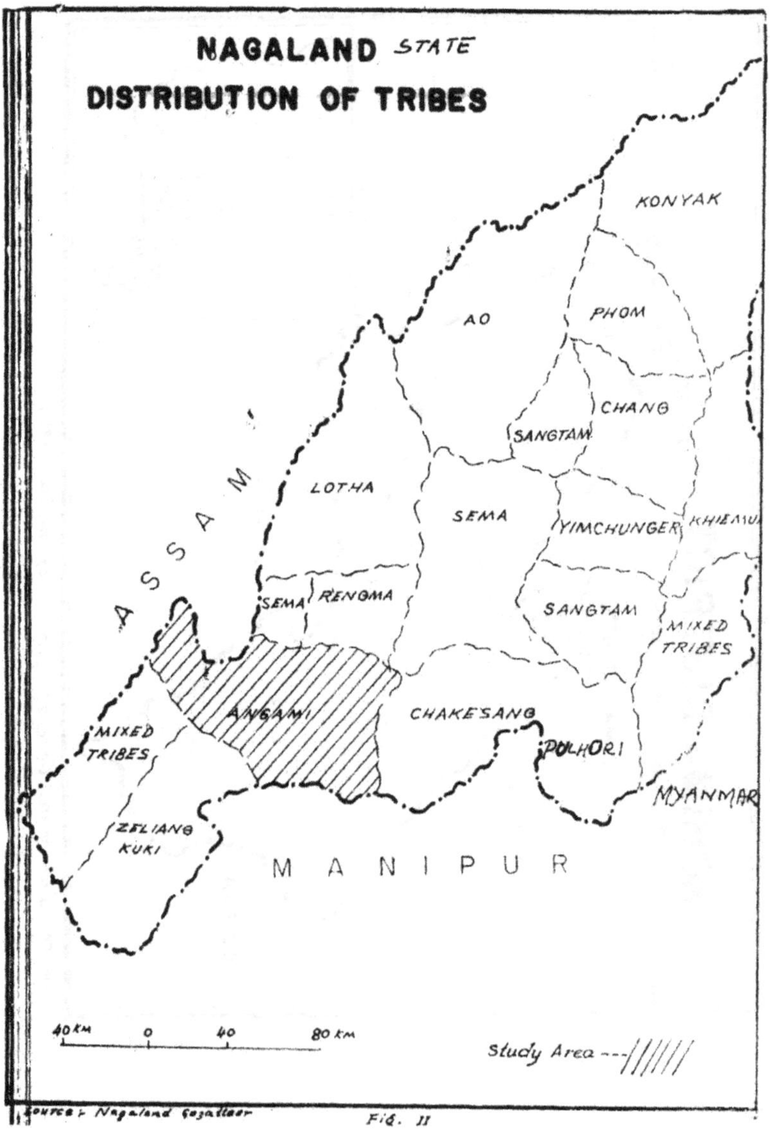

Source: Nagaland Gazetteer

Fig. II

ANGAMI SHIELD

ANGAMI SPEAR

ANGAMI CANE BASKETS

ORDINARY DAO AND HOE FOR DAILY USE